ally published in Italy under the title of:

HOW TO EAT OUT IN GERMANY
mese Editore s.r.l. – Via Virginia Agnelli
88 – 00151 Roma – Italy

English translation:
Mark White

Cover photo:
IFA-Bilderteam, Munich

© 2000 by Langenscheidt Publishers,
Inc. Maspeth, N.Y. 11378
Printed in Germany

Po

Menu

Ger

Gabrie

Orig

© G

of a d

as

LANGEN

NEW YORK · BERLIN · MU

Are you the kind of tourist who, wherever you go in the world, always ends up in the same kind of restaurant? What a shame! You could be missing out on some great culinary experiences. In Germany, for example, you can certainly find excellent Italian or French restaurants, but most of them adapt Italian or French dishes to German tastes, and the cheaper places may substitute local produce for authentic (and more expensive) imported ingredients. So if you have to look hard to find a good Italian or French restaurant, why not spend that energy seeking out a place serving good German, Austrian or Swiss food? Treat your tastebuds to some exciting new sensations.

German and Austrian cuisine suffers undeservedly from a harsh reputation abroad - where it has any reputation at all. However, bearing in mind the old maxim 'Don't knock it 'till you've tried it' most people will admit to knowing little about German cooking beyond sauerkraut and sausages. Let's consider the history of German cuisine and look at the circumstances in which it developed. First of all the climate can be one of the toughest in Europe and up until thirty or forty years ago most of the population was involved in manual labor. There was an obvious need for a high-calorie diet, which is why many dishes seem over-substantial to us today. However, modern German cooking has been influenced by the neighboring cuisines of France and Italy, not to mention a more widespread trend towards healthier, lighter eating. Often we find traditional recipes are adapted using vegetable oils instead of less easily-digested fats such as lard and butter, and sauces have become lighter and more delicate. Nowadays fresh ingredients are available all year round and in the winter it is no longer necessary to use leftovers or to 'beef up' dishes with bread and flour.

So do not fret about your cholesterol level, your liver, your digestion or your calorie intake. You can try all the regional specialties by looking for good restaurants which offer traditional cuisine cooked in modern, healthy, tasty ways. Prepare yourselves for dishes of different flavors and contrasts: sweet and savory; sweet and sour; hot and cold. As in most countries made up of many different regions, Germany, Austria and Switzerland do not have national cuisines as such, but rather many different regional variations, some of which have become much more widely known and been adopted as national dishes. This also allows us to cover these three countries (but only the German-speaking part of Switzerland) in one book: culinary traditions and techniques pay no heed to international boundaries, but depend on the similarities between areas and ways of life. For example, the *Spätzli* eaten in German-speaking Switzerland are the same as the *Spätzle* you will find in the Black Forest - the only difference being the spelling. Austria and Bavaria in southern Germany share many dishes and terms which are rare or even unknown in northern Germany. This book will introduce you to a selection of the best-known and most typical dishes. Should you have the chance to stay longer in any one region, you will discover even more for yourselves. So keep your eyes, mind and mouth open!

MAIN MEALS

The day begins with a hearty *Frühstück* (breakfast). Most people drink coffee, but tea or hot milk may be served and, in restaurants, fruit juice. Fresh bread rolls or slices of bread are served with butter and jam if you have a sweet tooth, or with butter, cheese and cold cuts if you prefer savory. You may also find cereals with milk or yoghurt if you prefer.

On holidays or special occasions a *zweites Frühstück* (lit. 'second breakfast') is usually served after Mass at about 11 o'clock. When the main element is beer, this is known as *Frühschoppen*.

Traditionally *Mittagessen* (lunch) is the most important meal of the day. In some areas it is known as *Mittagsmahl* or *Mittagsbrot*. The traditional starter *(Vorspeise)* is a basic meat broth which might contain noodles, egg, pieces of omelette, dumplings or meatballs. Otherwise the starter might be a vegetable soup such as cream of mushroom or tomato. Only in the last few years has there been a wider choice of starters. After the starter comes the *Hauptgericht* (main course). This will be meat or fish, often in a sauce and served with vegetables or salad and potatoes, rice or pasta. At the end of the meal there will be a dessert and sometimes a *Schnaps* or a liqueur, or perhaps coffee. Normally, however, coffee is not served until about four o'clock in the afternoon, with a slice of cake: *Kaffee und Kuchen*. If you prefer you can have tea or hot chocolate. Dinner is known as *Abendbrot* or *Abendessen*. The word *Abendbrot* (lit. 'evening bread') reveals that this is a light meal. It is often cold, comprising bread, cold cuts, cheese, salad, vegetables and perhaps a fried egg. Nowadays habits are changing. People who work all day may not have time for a hot meal at lunchtime, and prefer to eat their main meal in the evening. In restaurants there is no difference between the menu at lunch or dinner. Wine and beer are normally drunk at dinner.

You will find the restaurant menu divided into four sections: *Vorspeisen* (starters), *Hauptgerichte* (main dishes), *Beilagen* (side orders), and *Nachspeisen* (desserts)...if you're lucky to find one that simple! Most restaurants and their chefs are a little more adventurous and you may also find: *Suppen* (soups) or *aus dem Suppentopf* ('from the soup tureen'), *kleine Gerichte* (snacks), *Eierspeisen* (egg-based dishes), *Pfannengerichte* (pan-fried), *vom Rost* (broiled), *aus dem Ofen* (oven-cooked), *Spezialitäten* (specialties), *für unsere kleinen Gäste* ('for the little guests' - i.e. children's dishes), *kalte Gerichte* (cold dishes), *Salate* (salads), etc.

Bread. Unlike other places in Europe, bread is not traditionally eaten with meals. Most restaurants will provide some on request, but the waiter may look at you a little strangely. So take advantage of any opportunity you may have to eat bread at breakfast or any other time. Go into the bakeries *(Bäckerei)* to see and taste bread and rolls made in every way imaginable: with sesame, poppyseeds, sunflower seeds, nuts, onion, cheese, bacon and in every color from black to white. You absolutely must try the famous *Brezel*, perhaps hot and buttered. This is the pretzel's European cousin, a type of golden, crisp knotted ring, sprinkled with salt. It is most commonly found in Bavaria and Austria.

Salad. Until comparatively recently a salad would contain no more than a few soggy lettuce leaves, some tomato and cucumber, all swimming in water and vinegar. Nowadays the salads are delicious, and sometimes contain such ingredients as meat and egg, constituting a meal in themselves. Normally they are not dressed so you can add oil and vinegar to taste, or ask for the house *Dressing*, which is usually yoghurt- and herb-based.

Mealtimes. In the big cities restaurants and hotels no longer keep to set times. Traditionally, however, breakfast is not served after 9.30-10.00. Lunch may start as early as midday, and last orders are at about two o'clock. Coffee and cake are taken around four o'clock. If not, the evening meal may begin as early as 6.30, and in provincial areas kitchens can close at nine o'clock. If you dine in a pub or bar *(Bierkeller, Weinkeller, Bierstube, Weinstube, etc.)* you can remain seated until the place closes, even beyond midnight. Closing times differ from region to region, and there are special rules for popular tourist areas. In nearly all the big cities there are some places which are licensed to stay open throughout the night.

N.B. For those who don't know the language, one of the biggest problems when visiting a German-speaking country is that words are written running straight into one another, without helpful little spaces to separate the individual words! Therefore an item on the menu might look something like: 'chickeninaredwinesauce' or 'lambcutletswithFrenchfriesandcauliflowerinbechamelsauce'. The visitor's first task is to learn to recognize the keywords which will be found in the dictionary section at the back of the book.

WHERE TO EAT

When you are looking for somewhere to eat you will be pleased to find that restaurants display their menus outside. This will give you a good idea as to the food, and the prices, that you can expect to find inside. The prices include cover charge, service and VAT, so you know exactly how much you are spending. It is customary to leave a tip, but there are no hard and fast rules as to how much. Trust your judgment and tip according to the service received.

Bar (also **Nachtclub** or **Nightclub**): the German bar is the classic evening venue - something between a pub and a nightclub, somewhere people go to drink (watch out - it can be a bit pricey!), to listen to music and to meet girls who are there to encourage the clients to drink and spend even more. You will find precious little to eat.

Beisel: these are little Austrian restaurants dating from the nineteenth century, where you can find simple but tasty food which is still served with a mug of beer and eaten at large wooden tables.

Bistrot: similar to the *Café* (see below), bistrots were very popular in the '80s. Today they are mainly frequented by the young and so are fairly flexible, serving breakfast in the morning, snacks at lunchtime, cake in the afternoon and a meal complete with beer in the evening. They often have a menu of the day with a limited choice of dishes determined by the nationality of the cook and the preferences of the customers.

Café: this is where you can sit down for half an hour's rest and a cup of coffee. You will often find a sweet counter, especially when the *Café* is in a *Konditorei* (see below), where it can be very difficult to limit your choice to just one of the many treats on display! The typical *Café* is where middle-aged ladies meet with friends to chat over a cup of coffee and a cake. You can immediately tell a *Café* aimed at a younger crowd from its sign and the decor.

Gasthaus: originally a boarding house with a rough and ready restaurant attached. Some restaurants still use this term even if they no longer offer accommodation. They usually serve simple local food, in a basic setting and at mid-low prices.

Gasthof: a *Gasthaus* (see above) in the country.

Gaststätte: see *Restaurant* below.

Heuriger: a canopied restaurant serving wine from the previous grape harvest (which is also called *Heuriger*). Cold dishes may also be served, often to traditional music played by a small band.

Imbiß(stube), Pommesbude o **Würstchenbude:** these are snack bars or just kiosks serving all manner of German sausages, French fries or potato salad. The large number of Greek and Turkish immigrants have added their own specialties of *Gyros* and *Döner Kebab* respectively, to the traditional German snacks.

Kaffeehaus: an Austrian insititution. Here you can find numerous types of coffee, always accompanied by a glass of water which is constantly refilled. If you are hungry you can try savory snacks or the traditional cakes. This is where Austrians go to chat with friends, to see and be seen, to play cards, chess or billiards, to talk business or read the newspaper. The *Kaffeehaus* has a unique place in Austrian society.

Konditorei: the cakeshop. This may have a few tables where you can have a cup of coffee and one of the cakes from the counter. It may not be a particularly characterful place, but the cakes are excellent and ample compensation for somewhat bland surroundings.

Ratskeller: often the basements of Town Halls will house characteristic restaurants, traditional and welcoming, where local specialities are served at mid-high prices.

Restaurant, Gaststätte: the generic terms for restaurants of all types and classes. Look hard, perhaps with the help of a guide book or the advice of local people, for the right establishment to suit your needs. Keep in mind that first-class gourmet restaurants will often be heavily influenced by French cuisine. There are few top chefs who direct their energies to local specialties. You are more likely to find traditional fare in more characteristic restaurants which, even if a little touristy, have preserved the local cuisine.

Schanigarten: in Austria, the garden area in front of a bar or *Kaffeehaus*.

Weinkeller, Weinstube: the wine-drinker's equivalent of the *Bierkeller*. These are normally places of a certain class, offering a wide choice of wines, which you can enjoy with bread, cheese and savory bar snacks. Often they serve more substantial dishes too.

Würstelstand: roadside kiosks serving snacks of sausages and French fries. Common in Austria.

PUBS AND BIERKELLERS

These are known as *Kneipe, Bierhaus, Bierkeller, Lokal, Pinte, Stube* and *Stüberl* and they are normally cosy inviting places where you can drink beer, relax and chat with friends. Before choosing one you would do well to observe the sort of customers the place attracts, because this will give you some idea as to what the place will be like inside. However open-minded and tolerant you may consider yourself, you might not feel perfectly at home amongst German football fans whose team has just lost an important international, or a gang of skinheads who are not particularly fond of foreigners who do not speak their language or share their taste in hairstyles. There are bars frequented by students and tourists, local pubs where you can go for a quite nightcap, different bars for all ages. Given the large number of possibilities, you can have a quick look inside and if it does not appeal, simply move on to the next. In most of these places you can order something to line your stomach between beers. If you have chosen a characteristic place you might find some local delicacies.
In the summer months you will find a wonderful variant: the *Biergarten*. In these places the clientele is always very varied. Originally typical of Bavaria, the *Biergarten* have their origins in the beer cellars where, underneath the shadow of enormous chestnut trees, the beer kept longest. Nowadays you will find long wooden tables beneath the trees where you can enjoy a cool beer, although pretty much any place with a couple of tables outside has taken to calling itself a *Biergarten*. The real thing is only really found in Bavaria. At the weekend you will see entire families, on their way back from a day out, arriving at a *Biergarten* with snacks called *Brotzeit* (see also 'Gastronomic Terms') brought from home.

They will spend the rest of the afternoon here, in the company of their friends... and their beer. Do not worry if you have not brought anything to eat however, for anything you could want for a picnic will be available right there: from shank of pork with radishes to that old standby, potato salad.

HOLIDAYS AND FESTIVALS

The most famous German festival must be the *Oktoberfest*. The festivities take place in enormous buildings with great long medieval-style tables, to which the waiters carry five or six *Maßkrüge* (liter-glasses of beer) in each hand! There will normally be a band playing live music and an extremely high level of noise. If you are looking for a romantic, intimate venue for a date, on no account come here! Likewise if you are alone and not the type who enjoys getting involved in local customs. If, on the other hand, you are with a group of friends and you want to have fun, then this is the perfect place. But beware of the beer! The locals are used to this excess, for not only is there the *Oktoberfest* but every region also has its own beer festivals at various times throughout the year. Ask locally to find out when and where they are. They are also known as *Schützenfest* or *Kirchweih* or *Weinfest* in wine-producing regions.

SAUSAGES AND COLD CUTS

In Germany, Austria and Switzerland you will find an infinite number of sausages and cold cut meats. They are normally eaten on a slice of bread at breakfast or as a cold meal in the evening. There are also a great many dishes made with whole or sliced cooked sausages, or finished off with slices of a particularly flavorsome salami. In restaurants you can often order a platter of mixed cold cuts: an excellent way to familiarize yourself with local specialties. If you then want to buy your favorite, just ask the waiter for the exact name and make for the nearest butcher *(Metzgerei)* or well-stocked supermarket. Sausages, salamis and frankfurters exist in all forms, made from all types of meat: cooked, raw or fried. Each region has its own methods of production, so wherever you are, ask for the local specialty.

In recent years there has been a marked increase in the popularity of white meats, so the butchers have had to invent new types of sausages and cold cuts. This is a list of those you will most commonly find.

Bierwurst or **Bierschinken:** a large smoked sausage, coarse in texture, made with beef, pork and bacon.

Blockwurst: a type of salami, an inch thick, made with pork and beef, not too spicy.

Blutwurst: a kind of black pudding made with pork, bacon and pig's blood. It is eaten on bread. In some areas it is cut into fairly thick slices and pan-fried.

Bratwurst: a type of sausage which is broiled or fried, often sold by the roadside or at the *Imbiß* (see 'Where to Eat'). There are regional variations and *Bratwürste* come in all shapes and colors, and can be served with bread, various sauces, French fries, cabbage or on their own. They go particularly well with beer! (see also *Rostbratwurst*).

Debrecziner: a spicy pork frankfurter, which is boiled. Found throughout Austria in particular.

Fleischwurst: see *Schinkenwurst* below.

Frankfurter Würstchen: the classic frankfurter, a long, thin lightly-smoked pork sausage which is boiled and served in pairs *(ein Paar)* in a bread roll, topped with mustard.

Geflügelleberwurst: a type of liver sausage containing pâté made from the livers of various types of poultry, seasoned, cooked, and eaten spread on bread.

Katenwurst: a type of coarse salami, smoked in a particular way.

Krakauer: a strong-flavored, smoked pork and beef sausage, eaten boiled.

Landjäger: a small, flat sausage, made with raw smoked meat. Strong and spicy.

Leberwurst: a calves' liver and pork sausage. It is normally soft enough to spread on bread. Various types exist, from the rustic coarse version containing chunks of bacon, to the smoother, more refined version.

Lyoner Wurst: see *Schinkenwurst* below.

Mettwurst: a smoked sausage made of seasoned minced beef or pork.

Milzwurst: a sausage made with the meat and spleen from veal calves.

Nürnberger Rostbratwurst: a small *Bratwurst* with a strong flavor, cooked on the broiler.

Plockwurst: see *Blockwurst* above.

Preßsack: this sausage is made with meat from the head of a cow or pig which is boiled together with bacon rind and then squeezed into the animal's gut.

Puter in Aspik: stewed turkey and vegetables set in aspic. Eaten in slices.

Regensburger: a short and thick, pork or beef sausage.

Rostbratwurst: a top quality *Bratwurst,* i.e. made with prime cuts of meat, cooked on the broiler.

Schinkenspek: bacon and lean ham.

Schinkenwurst: a sausage made with lean pork, bacon and ham.

Schweinskopfsülze: aspic made from the pig's head and lean meat.

Sülzkotelett: a whole pork chop, boiled, set in aspic and served by the slice.

Sülzwurst: a mixture of meats and sometimes vegetables, in aspic, squeezed into an animal gut.

Teewurst: a smoked sausage, similar to a *Mettwurst* (see above), for spreading.

Weisswurst: a white sausage made with minced veal and fresh bacon, seasoned with parsley (see also 'Regional Dishes').

Wiener Würstchen: see *Frankfurter* above.

There is no doubt that Swiss cheeses are among the best in the world. However, excellent dairy produce can also be found in the Allgäuer Alpen mountains in Bavaria. So look out for the labels that bear this name, for it is regarded as a mark of quality.

Generally the strong-flavored cheeses are most popular in Germany, Austria and Switzerland. Natural-flavored cheeses are not produced. Cottage cheese, or quark, is made and flavored with herbs, onions and various spices.

Cheeses can be classified according to two criteria:
• according to the water content and, therefore the consistency:
Hart-Käse: hard cheese containing less then 40% water
Schnitt-Käse: cheese that can be sliced
Weich-Käse: soft cheese
Schmelz-Käse: soft, spreading cheese
Frisch-Käse: wet cheese
Sauermilch-Käse: sour milk cheese

• or according to the fat content:
Doppelrahm-Käse: double-cream cheese containing at least 60% fat
Vollfett-Käse: full-fat cheese
Halbfett-Käse: half-fat cheese
Mager-Käse: low-fat cheese containing no more than 10% fat.

Appenzeller: a hard, strong Swiss cheese.

Butterkäse: a soft, mild cheese, similar to butter, made with full-fat milk or cream.

Edelpilzkäse: a strong-flavored, semi-hard cheese which contains an edible mold.

Emmentaler: the famous Swiss cheese, hard and fatty, with holes as big as cherries and an aromatic flavor.

Graukäse: an Austrian cheese, similar to *Edelpilzkäse* (see above).

Greyerzer: Swiss gruyère cheese.

Handkäse: small round cheese, shaped by hand (hence the name), this is in fact a type of cottage cheese seasoned with cumin and salt. The marinaded version is known as *Handkäse mit Musik* (see 'Regional Dishes').

Harzer: similar to the *Handkäse* (see above), from the region of the Harz mountains.

Kochkäse: an Austrian product based on cottage cheese, salt and spices, cooked together.

Limburger: a soft, smelly cheese with a strong flavor and a greasy yellow/red surface. The stronger the smell, the more highly-prized the cheese.

Quark: cottage cheese, made in different ways, with a fat content ranging from *Magerquark* (low-fat) to *Sahnequark* (made with cream).

Raclette: a hard, strong Swiss cheese. It is melted on the fire before being eaten with boiled potatoes and vegetables (see also 'National Dishes').

Romadur: a soft cheese, rather spicy. Similar to *Limburger* (see above).

Sbrinz: a flavorsome hard Swiss cheese with small holes.

Schabziger: a hard Swiss cheese, made with herbs and spices, in the form of a cone. Matured and grated.

Schichtkäse: a cheese made with layers of cottage cheese with a varying fat content.

Tilsiter: a light yellow cheese with small holes and a strong flavor.

Weißkäse: a type of cottage cheese.

DRINKS

Beer

It is now believed that beer was first produced around 10,000 years ago in Asia, where the fermentation of grain was used in the making of drinks. In the past, the four basic ingredients (water, malt, hops and yeast) were essential for all beers. Nowadays, industrial processes mean that the flavor can be modified and developed in many different ways according to taste.

In Germany, beer names usually vary according to the place of origin or brewery.

Alt or **Altbier:** in German *alt* means old. Indeed, in the production of this type of beer, the oldest methods are employed to allow us a taste of yesteryear. This beer is produced in Westphalia and the Rhineland, and it was in the city of Düsseldorf that these methods were first perfected. The old city center is not called *Altstadt* after the beer, but it is true that Düsseldorf is almost one big brewery, and it is no coincidence that the city is known as "the biggest bar in the world!" *Alt* beers are bitters, with a high proportion of hops, giving them a light and delicately aromatic perfume. The alcoholic content of these beers is between 4° and 5°, and they are served cool, between 8° and 10°C, in 2 or 3cl glasses.

Bock: the color of these beers can vary from light amber to dark brown. The intensity of the malt flavor depends on the degree to which the grain is toasted. The flavor is full, aromatic and substantial. The alcohol is around 5.5°. These are the classic winter beers, served between 8° and 10°C, which go so well with hearty meals. *Bock* beers are traditionally served in a *Krug*, a ceramic tankard with a pewter lid designed to keep the aroma in. *Doppelbock* beers are noted for their stronger use of malt and are more alcoholic (between 5.7° and 6°). *Urbock* means 'original *Bock*' and is the name given to a beer produced according to a medieval recipe: it is a classic *Bock*, available as lager, stout and a special version only available in May. The latter is made at the beginning of spring and drunk before the arrival of summer.

Today all *Doppelbock* beers are denominated by the suffix -*ator* (from *Salvator*, the first beer named in this way) so as to make them more recognizable.

Dortmunder Export or **Dort:** in the second half of the last century, in a brewery in Dortmund, experiments were made into ways of transporting beer, without it suffering changes of characteristics and quality. The result was a lager called *Export* or *Dortmunder Export*, also known simply as *Dort*, which is similar to the classic original beer. It contains few hops, but is relatively strong (from 4° or 4.2° to 5°) and this is the secret of its good conservation. It is clear in color, the flavor tends towards the sweet, but it is not strongly flavored. Served between 10° and 12°C.

Festbier: these beers are produced in relatively small quantities for special occasions. They can be of any type, but are generally very full-bodied and alcoholic.

Kölsch: a beer with ancient origins, produced only in the city of Cologne, which is still the only place where it can be drunk, as it does not take kindly to transportation. It is a crisp lager, with just the right hint of bitterness, and a light flavor of hops. Its alcohol content is 3.7°. Served not too cold at about 14°C, in *Stangen*: narrow cylindrical glasses, of very thin glass containing 0.2 or 0.3l.

Malzbier: a sweet dark beer with a high malt content, with little or no alcohol. Drunk principally by children and pregnant women.

Märzenbier: literally 'March beer', i.e. the beer traditionally produced at the beginning of spring which was ready for consumption by the end of August. Nowadays it is made all year round and has a color anything between light and dark gold, almost amber. It has a dry, full malted flavor, rather substantial without being strong. The alcohol content varies between 3.8° and 4.5°. It is served chilled, between 9° and 11°C.

Münchner: this is what is served if you order simply: *ein Dunkles* ('stout') or *ein Helles* ('a lager'). The former is dark brown in color, with a malty taste, but not sweet. It varies between 4° and 5° in alcohol. It is not served chilled, but at 14° to 16°, in a *Maßkrug*, a beer jug containing one liter. It can also be served in a smaller glass containing 0.4 or 0.5l *(eine Halbe)*.
The lager version is golden in color, with a crisp, somewhat bitter taste, due to the low levels of hops. It is served at a lower temperature, between 10° and 12°C.

Pilsener, Pils or **Pilsner:** three names for a lager, originally from the town of Pilsen, which is now in the Czech Republic, although it was actually invented by a Bavarian brewer. The alcohol content ranges from 3.8° to 4°. It is served at about 10°C in 0.3 or 0.4l glasses. In Germany there are also darker versions.

Rauchbier: today only four breweries produce this kind of 'smoked' beer: three are in Bamberg, the other in Nuremberg. Its unique flavor was created by an unintentional error in the malt-drying process. Its color ranges from amber to copper. It has a malty taste, with a pleasantly smoky quality. It contains 4.5° alcohol. It is served between 12° and 14°C and goes particularly well with smoked foods.

Weizenbier: this type of beer is not made with barley alone, but rather with a mixture of varying proportions of barley and other grains. It is noted for its abundant frothiness; in fact barmen have had to develop a specific technique for pouring it into the glass. The most famous *Weizenbier* are as follows:
Berliner Weiße: slightly acidic flavour, an aftertaste of lactic fermentation, very gassy, and slightly bitter; a light beer (2.6°), traditionally served at 7-9°C in a wide cup with a drop of raspberry syrup.
Weizenbier or *Weißbier*: the classic grain beer from the southern regions. There are two variations: *Hefeweizen* and *Hefefrei*, meaning with or without yeast respectively. The former is clear and golden, while the latter is darker and cloudier. It has a malty taste, with just a hint of hops. It also exists as a stout, *Weizendunkel*. These beers contain 4°

alcohol and are served chilled, between 6° and 8°C in half-liter glasses.

Two types of beer have a greater alcohol strength (up to 6°) and a stronger flavor: *Weizenbock* and *Weizendoppelbock*.

Austrian beers: Austria has been a wine-producing region since Roman times, but since the Middle Ages it has been in competition with beer. The most famous brands are: *Gösser, Schwechater, Villacher, Reininghaus Bier* and *Stiegl-Bräu.*

WINE

Despite a climate which is hardly perfect for the cultivation of vines, **Germany** manages to produce some excellent wines which are amongst the best in the world. In some river valleys, in particular those of the Rhine, the Moselle, the Saar and the Ruhr, the climate is very mild and the slopes are at a perfect angle for growing vines, allowing for the right balance between sugar and acidity. Viticulture was introduced to the Moselle region by the Romans. The most commonly used grape varieties for making white wine are *Riesling, Müller-Thurgau, Silvaner* and *Traminer. Portugieser* and *Spätburgunder* are used in the production of red wines. The majority of red wine, which is produced in much smaller quantites than white, comes from the Ahr valley near Bonn and Franconia. Franconian wines, which are mainly white, have characteristic low, round bottles, called *Bocksbeutel*, which are unique to this region.

Wines are divided into three categories: *Tafelwein* (table wine), *Qualitätswein eines bestimmten Anbaugebietes b. A.* (guaranteed good-quality wine) and *Qualitätswein b. A. mit Prädikat* (guaranteed top-quality wine). *Kabinett, Spätlese, Auslese, Beerenauslese, Trockenbeerenauslese* denote the length of the aging process: the older they are, the greater the quantity of naturally occurring sugar. Be warned that only for the *QmP* category is the addition of sugar forbidden! In recent years there has been an increase in the production of dry wines. In Germany the harvest (*Lese*, in German) takes place between September and the end of October; to make *Spätlese* ('late harvest') or *Eiswein* (the highly-prized 'ice-wine') the harvest can take place as late as December. Sparkling wine is known as *Sekt*.

The following is a list of the major wine-producing regions, and the characteristics of the wine from each area:

Ahr: red wine
Baden: the great variety of soils and grape varieties allows for the production of intensely flavored wines
Franken: dry wine, rich bouquet
Mittelrhein: fresh, fruity wine
Mosel, Saar, Ruwer: light, fresh, clear wines with rich bouquets
Nahe: light, slightly sweet, fruity
Rheingau: the soil and climate are ideal for the production of excellent wines; rich bouquets, slightly fruity
Rheinhessen (Hesse): a great variety of red and white wines; light but intensely flavored
Rheinpfalz (Palatinate): heavy-bodied, fiery

DRINKS

The **Austrians** also produce predominantly white wines.
These tend to be stronger and more aromatic than German
wines. There is also a long tradition of robust sweet wines.
Lower Austria is home to the three most important wine-
producing regions: the Wienerwald hills, the Wachau-
Kamptal region, and the area between Vienna and the Czech
border. Good wines are also produced in Stiria and around
the Neusiedler See.

Swiss wine is good quality, and will accompany a meal well.
Again, mostly white wines are produced, although there are
some reds.

Soft Drinks

Alsterwasser: see *Radler* below

Apfelsaftschorle or **Apfelschorle:** apple juice diluted with
mineral water.

G'spritzter: wine spritzer.

Radler: beer and lemonade shandy, drunk especially in the
summer, known in the north as *Alsterwasser*, in the south as
Radler.

Russe: a mixture of *Weizenbier* and lemonade.

Spezi: a mixture of Coca-Cola and orangeade.

Weinschorle: simply wine and mineral water.

SPIRITS AND LIQUERS

In places where the sun rarely shines, sometimes we need a little something to warm us up from the inside. As well as bitters and liqueurs, the most popular liquors are *Schnäpse* or *Klare*, clear, strong double-distilled spirits, often served ice-cold. They are drunk after dinner, or along with beer: first you down a glass of *Schnaps* to warm yourself up, then you drink your beer. *Korn* is a popular type of Schnaps made from grain.

COFFEE

The coffee drunk in **Austria** is generally quite strong and aromatic and is often served not in cups but in little bowls. There are various ways of making coffee, but the most common are as follows: *Großer Schwarzer* (double espresso), *Kleiner Schwarzer* (regular espresso), *Kleiner Brauner* (coffee with a dash of milk), *Großer Brauner* (similar to a cappuccino), *Nußschwarzer* or *Neger* (mocha), *Einspänner* (black coffee topped with whipped cream), *Melange* (white coffee topped with whipped cream) and *Türkischer Kaffee* (Turkish coffee).

In **Germany** filter coffee is most commonly drunk *schwarz* (black), *mit Zucker* (with sugar) or *mit Milch* (with milk). Concentrated milk is often used, which contains 10% fat. Coffee is drunk in the morning with breakfast and in the afternoon with a slice of cake. If you go to a *Café* (see 'Where to Eat') it will be served in *eine Tasse* (a cup) or in *ein Kännchen* (a two-cup coffee pot). In more modern cafés you may also be able to order an espresso or a cappuccino. Do not be too surprised to find your cappuccino topped with whipped cream or some other exotic extra.

The first factory for extracting sugar from sugar beet was only set up in 1801. Before this, honey and dried fruit were widely used in cakes and pastries which were only made for special occasions, as imported cane sugar was too expensive. Nowadays there is an infinite variety of sweets, cakes and tarts. In many *Konditoreien* (see 'Where to Eat') there are tables where you can sit with a cup of coffee and taste whatever you choose from the delights displayed at the counter. The most popular dessert amongst Germans, however, is ice cream, which is often served with something hot, perhaps a fruit pie, a hot chocolate or an apple strudel.

Apfelkompott or **Apfelmus:** an apple purée, which is not eaten only as a dessert, but also, in some regions, as a side dish with, for example, *Kartoffelpuffer* (see 'National Dishes').

Apfelkuchen: apple pie, of which there are a thousand varieties.

Apfelstrudel: see *Strudel* below.

Arme Ritter: bread, soaked in beaten egg and milk, fried and dusted with sugar and cinnamon, sometimes served with apple purée.

Auszogne: leavened pastries, fried in oil and sprinkled with icing sugar.

Bayerische Creme: the world-famous Bavarian custard, almost as well-known as *Knödel*. In Bavaria, where it is called

Rahmsulz, for generations it has always concluded the menu on great occasions such as weddings, christenings etc. The custard is cooked in a bainmarie and contains eggs, sugar, gelatine and the principal ingredient: cream.

Berliner Pfannkuchen or **Krapfen:** donuts, filled with jam.

Bienenstich: a cake with a buttercream and almond, or a vanilla egg-custard filling.

Birne Helene: half a pear with vanilla ice cream and chocolate sauce.

Biskuitrolle: a type of Swiss roll. A thin layer of sponge cake, covered with whipped cream and rolled up. The roll itself is then covered with whipped cream and decorated. Many varieties exist using fruit, chocolate or nuts.

Bratapfel: baked apple, eaten at Christmastime. Sadly, the scarcity of coal-fired ovens nowadays means that this traditional dish is almost forgotten.

Brunsli: biscuits, traditionally made at Christmastime in Switzerland. Made with sugar, almonds, chocolate icing, egg white and cherry liqueur.

Buchteln: sweet dumplings with various fillings.

Butterkuchen: a griddle cake, spread with butter, sugar and almonds. Best eaten when still warm.

Dampfnudel: a sweet leavened dumpling steamed in a well-sealed saucepan. In the south it is served with a warm vanilla sauce. When it is fresh it is soft and warm to the core; if not fresh it is like chewing a brick, and impossilbe to swallow - complain immediately! In the north they are slightly different, more like sweet *Knödel* and served with cooked fruit.

Errötende Jungfrau: literally translated, this means 'blushing virgin.' It is a classic German dessert with many regional variations. It consists of alternate layers of milk jelly and strawberries and raspberries.

Flammeri: a sort of semolina pudding, served cold.

Frankfurter Kranz: this consists of a ring cake, cut in half horizontally and filled with cream made with butter, cream and egg yolk. It is topped with candied cherries and almond crunch. It so rich and filling that one slice is as much as most people can manage.

Fürst-Pückler-Eis: probably the most famous ice cream dish in Germany, even if it consists of 'only' alternate layers of strawberry, chocolate and vanilla flavor ice cream. (A combination known as Neapolitan ice cream in Britain.) The homemade version is delicious.

Germknödel: in southern Germany and in Austria these balls of leavened dough are filled with plums and coated in butter, sugar and poppy seeds.

Götterspeise: this dessert is based around a fruit jelly which may be served with whipped cream, or layered with custard, fruit, chocolate, etc. When it is layered with apple purée (in northern Germany) it is known as *Verschleiertes Bauernmädchen* (i.e. 'veiled peasant girl').

Guglhupf: a type of donut made with rum, raisins, and hazlenuts or chopped almonds.

Kaiserschmarrn: probably the most famous Austrian dessert, this is a crêpe made with eggs, flour, milk and sugar. Just before it sets in the pan, it is cut into slices with a fork and covered with raisins and icing sugar. It might be served with a fruit purée.

Käsekuchen: a shortcrust pastry tart filled with cottage cheese, soured cream, eggs and sugar. Sometimes raisins or pieces of fruit may be added.

Käsesahnetorte: a sponge base spread with a cream made from eggs, cream and cottage or cream cheese and jelly.

Kipferl or **Kipfel:** crescent-moon shaped biscuits.

Kirschstreusel: see *Streuselkuchen* below.

Kolatschen: sweets made from leavened dough, and containing various fillings.

Königskuchen: a simple cake made with flour, eggs, sugar and butter, with the addition of raisins, candied fruit and almonds.

Krapfen: see *Berliner* above.

Lebkuchen: bread flavored with honey, made originally in Nuremberg. At Christmas it is found everywhere, in every shape and variation imaginable.

Lebkucheneis: an excellent ice cream from Nuremberg made, believe it or not, from leftover *Lebkuchen*.

Leckerli: biscuits made with honey, dried fruits and almonds. A speciality of Basel.

Liebesknochen: 'A bone as sweet as love': or rather, a delicious chocolate-coated biscuit.

Linzer Torte: a tart made with chopped hazelnuts and covered with a layer of raspberry jam.

Marillenknödel: apricots wrapped in potato pastry and baked in the oven. Before being served they are rolled in breadcrumbs which have been browned in butter. If plums are used instead, the dish is known as *Zwetschgenknödel*.

Marmorkuchen: A ring-shaped marble cake. The dough is divided in two; one half is then colored with cocoa powder, while the other remains white. The two halves are then worked together to give the marble effect.

Millirahmstrudel or **Milchrahmstrudel:** a *Strudel* (see below) stuffed with cottage cheese, cream and raisins.

Mohnstriezel: a plait of leavened dough with poppy seeds. At Christmastime it is enriched with chopped hazelnuts, raisins and candied fruit.

Mohrenkopf: small, but delicious, this 'Moor's head' is a soft meringue coated with a very thin layer of bitter chocolate, found in the *Konditoreien* (see 'Where to Eat'), and also in the supermarket. There is another sweet of the same name which is a chocolate meringue with whipped cream.

Mohr in Hemd: a steamed chocolate pudding.

Mozartkugeln: these famous sweets from Salzburg are balls of chocolate filled with marzipan, nougat and rum. The perfect souvenir to take home, if you manage not to eat them on the way, that is!

Napfkuchen: see *Guglhupf* above.

Ofenschlupfer: a dessert made with leavened dough.

Palatschinken: delicately-flavored filled crêpes, often served with ice cream or whipped cream.

Pfefferkuchen: peppered bread.

Pfirsich Melba: peach melba: half a peach with vanilla ice cream, melba sauce and whipped cream.

Pflaumenkuchen: see *Zwetschgendatschi* below.

Printen: see *Lebkuchen* above. These differ only in shape.

Prinzregentorte: a sponge cake, cut into five or six layers each of which is spread with chocolate buttercream. The cake is coated with more chocolate buttercream and then covered with chocolate icing.

Rahmsulz: see *Bayerische Creme* above.

Rehrücken: chocolate cake, covered with chocolate icing and decorated with almonds. The name is that of a meat dish because it loosely resembles a larded saddle of venison.

Reis Trauttmansdorff: the Trauttmansdorffs are an ancient noble dynasty. This pudding of creamed rice and candied fruit was created in honor of one of the family.

Rhabarber-Kompott: rhubarb is very popular in Germany as dessert. This dish is a compôte, often served with hot vanilla custard.

Rohrnudel: a long leavened pastry.

Rote Grütze: imported from Scandinavia, this is now one of the most popular summer desserts, thanks to the flavors of the fresh fruit. The juice or purée of raspberries and redcurrants (or any other fruit, as long as it is red in color) is set with starch or gelatine, and served with single cream.

Rumtopf: fruit steeped in rum and served as a topping over ice cream, etc.

Sachertorte: one of the most famous desserts in the world, this is a triumph of chocolate with a filling of apricot jam, all of which is encased in chocolate icing.

Salzburger Nocklern: a soufflé made with only egg white, sugar, butter and a little flour.

Scheiterhaufen: a dessert consisting of layers of white bread and fruit, baked in the oven.

Schnecke: spirals of puff pastry, sometimes with raisins.

Schwarzwälder Kirschtorte: the original Black Forest Gateau: a layered chocolate sponge cake, filled with whipped cream and cherry jam, covered with flakes of dark chocolate.

Schweinsohren: sweet puff pastries which resemble pigs' ears, hence their name.

Streuselkuchen: a leavened cake covered with *Streusel*, i.e. pieces of shortcrust pastry. If cherries are spread underneath the pastry the cake is called *Kirschstreusel*. Other fruits can also be used

Strudel: very finely rolled pastry, or puff pastry, with a filling such as apple, raisins etc. Often served with ice cream or whipped cream.

Vanilleeis mit heißen Himbeeren: vanilla ice cream with a topping of hot rasberry sauce - delicous!

Vanillekipferl: vanilla-flavoured biscuits in the shape of a crescent moon.

Verschleiertes Bauermädchen: see *Götterspeise* above.

Waffel: these waffles are normally sold freshly-made at stands by the roadside. They may be served with ice cream, whipped cream, fruit and/or chocolate.

Windbeutel: cream puff.

Zuger Kirschtorte: the Swiss city of Zug is besieged by cherry orchards, and it is home to this cherry speciality: a cake of many layers of sponge alternating with layers of hazelnut paste, cherry jam and buttercream.

Zwetschgendatschi or **Zwetschgenkuchen:** a tart made with ripe plums on a shortcrust or leavened pastry base, served with whipped cream or ice cream.

Zwetschgenknödel: see *Marillenknödel* above.

GASTRONOMIC TERMS

Apfelmus or **Apfelkraut:** apple purée; in some regions this is eaten on the side with meat or fried foods. *Apfelkraut* is more similar to jam.

Auflauf: a soufflé made with potato, vegetables and/or meat or fish. There are also sweet varieties.

Aufschnittplatte: a plate of cold cuts and sausages.

Belegtes Brot or **Brötchen** or **Semmel:** a slice of bread or a bread roll with cold cuts or cheese.

Blau: a way of cooking fish. The fish is poached and then boiling water and vinegar are poured over it, turning the skin blue.

Brotzeit: a magic word to the people of Munich. This is a snack which can be eaten at any time of day, and anywhere - even outside, picnic-style. Any number of specialities might be eaten, such as *Leberkäs, Weißwürste, Wurstsalat, Radi, Obazda* (see also 'Regional Dishes.')

Durchgebraten: see *Steak* below.

Eintopf: a thick, rich soup made with potato, vegetables and/or meat. An all-in-one dish.

Englisch: see *Steak* below.

Essigkren: horseradish sauce (Austria). An accompaniment to meat or vegetables. Hot.

GASTRONOMIC TERMS

Flambiert: flambé. Rum or liquer is poured over the dish (normally a dessert, but also some meat dishes), set alight and served in flames. The alcohol burns off, imparting a certain flavor to the dish.

Florida: a dish containing pieces of fruit - pineapple, banana or mandarin.

Gärtnerinart: denotes dishes with vegetables.

Gebackene Erbsen: drops of bread dough fried and cooked in stock.

Geröstete: literally means 'roast'. On its own it refers to pan-fried parboiled potatoes (Austria).

Gerstel: a broth containing a particular kind of grated noodle (Austria).

Grün: means fresh, raw, savory, or dried (e.g. bacon, herrings etc) i.e. *not* smoked. Also means steamed fish.

Grüne Soße: a specialty of the Hesse region: a green sauce made with yoghurt, cream, lemon and herbs.

Hausfrauenart: 'homestyle'.

Hausmacherart: 'home-cooking'.

Hawaii: see *Florida* above. A *Toast Hawaii* is a slice of toast topped with, amongst other things, a slice of pineapple and melted cheese.

GASTRONOMIC TERMS

Holländische Soße: a kind of bechamel sauce widely used with vegetables, potatoes, cauliflower, asparagus, leeks, etc. Sometimes served with meat or fish.

Jägerart: this term, the equivalent of the Italian '*alla cacciatora*', or French '*chasseur*', means that the dish includes a sauce containing mushrooms.

Kaltschale: a cold fruit purée. Served in the summer as a soup starter or a dessert.

Knödel: in southern Germany and Austria this term commonly indicates both dumplings and meatballs. If the type is not specified, it means potato dumplings served on the side.

Medaillons: loin-cut medallions of meat.

Medium: see *Steak* below.

Mehlspeise: flour-based dishes. In Austria there are sweets that go by this name, although they do not contain flour.

Mett: minced pork, eaten raw, spread on bread and dressed with onion and seasoning.

Müllerinart: a term used to describe a dish (usually fish) in breadcrumbs, fried in butter and brushed with melted butter.

Nockerln: egg and flour-based dumplings.

Ofenkartoffel: potatoes baked in foil, served with herb butter or soured cream.

Petersilienkartoffeln: boiled pototoes garnished with parsley.

Pfannengerichte: this means 'pan-fried'.

Pfannkuchen: this normally indicates a pancake or omelet. It can be sweet, with a filling of sugar, syrup or fruit, or savory, fried with cheese, vegetables or meat. The *Berliner Pfannkuchen* on the other hand, is a jam donut.

Rübenkraut: a sugarbeet jam. In sugarbeet-growing areas, such as the Rhineland, it is eaten on the side, spread on wholemeal bread.

Sauer: literally 'sour, sharp, acidic' this normally indicates the use of vinegar or a sharp flavor in a dish.

Schnitte: 'a slice'. This normally indicates a slice of bread topped with, amongst other things, meat and cheese.

Senf: mustard. There are several varieties: *süßer Senf* (sweet mustard), *milder Senf* (mild mustard), *mittelscharfer Senf* (mid-hot mustard) and *scharfer* or *Löwensenf* (hot mustard).

Spezialität des Hauses: the house speciality.

Steak: one of the easier-to-understand items on the menu, but what if the waiter asks how you like yours done?

englisch: rare/underdone
medium: medium
durchgebraten: well done.

Suppentopf, aus dem: literally means 'from the soup tureen', and indicates soups and broths.

Tartar(beefsteak): raw minced steak eaten on bread with onion and seasoning.

Zigeunerart: 'gypsy-style', this term describes spicy dishes containing bell peppers and onion.

In Austria, Germany and Switerland a meal normally consists of meat or fish, served with vegetables or salad and potatoes, rice or noodles. Therefore it is difficult to describe a typical dish, for the three parts vary according to the whim of the chef. You can either use this book to identify the various items, like completing a jigsaw puzzle, or you can try to work out what the main ingredient is, and just take pot luck with the rest. In the more economical restaurants you will often find *Eintopf* (soup) or soufflé, the ingredients of which may not be easily identified. You may like to warm yourself up with a soup to start, and finish your meal with a dessert. We would suggest that if you wanted to skip one of the courses, leave out the soup, and indulge in a large helping of pudding. However, it can be difficult to find local specialities as the cuisines of neighboring countries, Italy, France and eastern Europe in particular, as well as changes in the customers' eating habits have had a profound influence on modern cuisine.

AUSTRIA

Backhendl: baked chicken in breadcrumbs.

Beinfleisch: boiled beef.

Beuscherl: calves' lungs, heart and spleen boiled and dressed in vinegar.

Bruckfleisch: stew of offal (heart, liver, spleen etc) and vegetables, cooked in red wine with cumin and sweet marjoram.

Edelgulasch: veal *Gulasch* (see below) with the addition of cream.

Fischbeuschlsuppe: vegetable soup containing fish roe.

Fleckerlsuppe: broth with noodles.

Fleischknödel: see *Frikadellen* below.

Frittatensuppe or **Flädlesuppe:** a simple broth containing shreds of omelet.

Gebackene Schwammerl: baked mushrooms in breadcrumbs.

Grießnockerlnsuppe: a soup containing *Nockerln*, dumplings made with semolina, eggs and butter.

Gulasch: originally from Hungary, goulash has been adopted as a national dish by both Austria and Germany. It is a beef stew containing paprika, served with lashings of gravy. Can also be made with pork or veal.

Gulaschsuppe: the gravy from the *Gulasch* (see above) can be served as a starter or *Eintopf* (see 'Gastronomic Terms'). As an *Eintopf* it is enriched with potato, bell peppers and other vegetables.

Jungfernbraten: roast loin of pork, flavored with cumin.

Kaiserfleisch: a pork or veal chop in brine, boiled and served in its cooking gravy with vegetables and horseradish.

Karfiol auf Wiener Art: baked cauliflower served in a cream-based sauce with tripe and anchovies.

Kochsalat: leaves cooked in a flour-based sauce.

Krenfleisch: porkmeat, including the rind, boiled and served with horseradish.

Lungenbraten: loin of beef in a cream sauce.

Paprika-Huhn: chicken in tomato and paprika sauce, served with pasta and rice.

Radi: a horseradish cut in a very fine spiral and salted to make it 'weep', rendering it less spicy.

Rostbraten Esterhazy: steaks fried in soured cream flavored with capers and lemon.

Tafelspitz: boiled top-quality beef, often served with horseradish.

Tellerfleisch: beef or pork, boiled then sliced, served in the cooking juices.

Tiroler Gröstl: pieces of boiled meat, potatoes and egg fried together in a pan.

Tiroler Knödel: a potato dumpling stuffed with bacon (see *Kartoffelklöße* below).

Wiener Schnitzel: fried veal or pork in breadcrumbs. A classic dish, also found in Germany, offered in nearly every restaurant. Usually served with salad and French fries.

Zigeunerspieß: a skewer of mixed meats, onion and roast bell peppers.

GERMANY

Bauchstecherla: see *Schupfnudeln* below.

Béchamelkartoffeln: boiled, sliced potatoes immersed in bechamel sauce. Often eaten as a side order when the main dish is quite dry.

Bismarckhering mit Kartoffelsalat: a pickled herring fillet, eaten cold with potato salad.

Blaukraut: another name for *Rotkohl* (see below).

Bœuf Stroganoff: fillet of beef stewed in a sauce containing cognac and/or cream, often served on buttered rice. Originally an Eastern European dish.

Brathähnchen, Brathuhn, Brathendl, or **Broiler:** roast chicken. Found everywhere in the more economical restaurants and *Imbißtuben,* often served with French fries.

Bratkartoffeln: potatoes which are parboiled, then pan-fried. Eaten as a side dish or with a fried egg or salad as an all-in-one meal. This dish is at its best when the potatoes are full of flavor and boiled the day before.

Bratwurst mit Pommes frites: the classic German fast food found at an *Imbiß* (see 'Where to Eat'): fried or grilled sausage and French fries.

Broiler: see *Brathähnchen* above.

Bubespitzle or **Buwespitz:** see *Schupfnudeln* below.

Buletten: see *Frikadellen* below.

Camembert gebacken mit Preiselbeeren: probably a recipe of French origin. Wedges of camembert are coated in breadcrumbs, deep fried and served with cranberries. Served in many places as an appetizer or a snack.

Champignoncremesuppe: cream of mushroom soup. Creamy soups are very popular in Germany.

Chateaubriand: a thick loin cut of beef, fried with herb butter or other sauces, often served with French fries.

Eier in Senfsoße: hard-boiled eggs in mustard accompanied by new potatoes.

Eiersalat: a hard-boiled egg salad with mayonnaise. Often includes peas and various spices.

Eisbein mit Sauerkraut: a pig's trotter in brine, cooked and served with sauerkraut and mashed potatoes or mushy peas.

Erbensuppe: when this soup is made only with peas, whether puréed or in a broth, it is served as an appetizer. Often however, it takes the form of a true *Eintopf* (see 'Gastronomic Terms') with the addition of potatoes, stewing meat, bacon, onions and/or other vegetables. This is a classic dish traditionally made at folk festivals.

Fingernudeln: see *Schupfnudeln* below.

Fischfrikadellen: in times past people who lived in coastal areas used up the previous day's leftover fish by making fish balls. Today, of course, fresh fish is used. It is chopped finely and mixed with stale bread and pan-fried. The balls are served with a potato salad on the side.

Fleischbrühe (Klare): a simple meat broth which was traditionally served as an appetizer at Sunday lunch. Today this tradition is somewhat obsolete, although most restaurants will serve a soup of some kind. According to local custom it may be embellished with noodles, slivers of pancake, dumplings or various kinds of meatball (see *Markklößchensuppe, Flädle, Leberknödel* in 'Regional Dishes').

Fleischpflanzerl: see *Frikadellen* below.

Forelle blau: trout poached in water and vinegar, which turns the fish blue. Excellent with boiled new potatoes.

Französische Zwiebelsuppe: see *Zwiebelsuppe* below.

Frikadellen: meatballs made with ground meat and stale bread. Depending on the region they are also known as *Buletten, Fleischknödel* and *Fleischpfanzerl*.

Gänsebraten: the best recipes for this dish originated in the eastern areas of Germany, where there are enormous goose and turkey farms. Stuffed roast goose is the classic Christmas dinner and the red cabbage served alongside complements it wonderfully.

Gefüllte Paprikaschoten: bell peppers stuffed with ground meat and/or rice, cooked in tomato sauce, usually served with boiled potatoes or rice.

Gefüllte Kalbsmedallions: veal medallions stuffed with mushrooms, onions etc. Served with boiled potatoes or rice.

Grumbeerküchle: see *Kartoffelpuffer* below.

Hammelkoteletts auf grünen Bohnen: fried mutton chops served with string beans.

Hasenpfeffer: a fricassé of hare, marinaded in pepper, other spices and red wine, braised and served in a sauce based on the marinade.

Heringssalat: a salad of herrings in brine, with beetroot, apple, gherkins and onion, dressed with mayonnaise or soured cream.

Hühnerfrikassee: chicken breast fricassé was once a very refined dish, reserved for special feast days. Nowadays simpler recipes are followed, using pieces of tongue and mushroom served on a bed of rice.

Jägerschnitzel: veal escalope 'alla cacciatora' or 'chasseur' i.e. with a mushroom sauce.

Kaiserschnitzel: veal cutlet in cream.

Kalbsfrikassee: the real veal fricassé is a very elaborate dish; it is well worth trying if you get the chance.

NATIONAL DISHES

Kartoffelgratin: potato gratin.

Kartoffelklöße: *Knödel* of boiled potato. There are many varieties: *halb und halb* (half boiled potato, half grated raw potato); with egg; with semolina; filled with bread and bacon (*Speckklöße*) or prunes. In southern Germany and Austria they are called *Knödel*.

Kartoffelplätzchen: see *Kartoffelpuffer* below.

Kartoffelpuffer: also known as *Kartoffelplätzchen, Grumbeerküchle, Reiberdatschi* or *Reibekuchen* these are fritters of grated raw potato. In Bavaria they are eaten with sauerkraut or apple sauce; in the Rhineland they are served on a slice of wholemeal bread and spread with sugarbeet syrup; in Thuringia they are covered in blueberries. Eating *Kartoffelpuffer* is one way to get to know the flavors of the local cuisine.

Kartoffelpüree: mashed potato is a much-loved side dish. It may sometimes include other vegetables, herbs or even fruit.

Kartoffelsalat: potato salad. Served cold with a mayonnaise or oil and vinegar dressing, or warm with chopped onion and bacon. One of the mainstays of German cuisine, it is found in every region and many variations. It is such a popular dish that some cheaper restaurants, diners and in particular the *Imbißstuben* (see 'Where to Eat') which sell fried foods keep their *Kartoffelsalat* in five- or ten-kilo containers. (Obviously such potato salad may not be of the highest quality, however.) When homemade it is truly delicious and well-worth tasting.

Kartoffelsuppe: an appetizer or *Eintopf* (see 'Gastronomic Terms') based around boiled puréed potatoes.

Kasseler mit Sauerkraut: a smoked pork chop in brine with sauerkraut.

Knödel: see *Kartoffelklöße* above.

Kohlrouladen or **Krautwickel:** cabbage rolls stuffed with ground meat.

Königinpastete: vol-au-vent, filled with chicken, mushroom etc. Served as appetizers.

Königsberger Klopse or **Saure Klopse:** meatballs made with ground meat, stale bread and anchovies, cooked in a flour-based sauce containing butter and capers.

Krabbensalat or **Krabbencocktail:** in northern Germany prawn cocktail is a very popular appetizer. The prawns come from the North Sea and have a strong flavor.

Krautsalat: a white cabbage salad with cumin and sometimes pieces of crispy bacon.

Krautwickel: see *Kohlrouladen* above.

Linsensuppe: lentil soup.

Ochsenbrust mit Meerrettich: brisket of beef with horseradish.

Ochsenschwanzsuppe: oxtail soup. Often served as an appetizer. When potatoes, vegetables and other pieces of meat are added, it becomes an *Eintopf* (see 'Gastronomic Terms').

Paprikaschnitzel: see *Zigeunerschnitzel* below.

Quarknudeln: egg and durum wheat pasta, pan-fried with cottage cheese.

Ragout fin: puff pastry filled with a veal and cream sauce.

Ranzenstecher: see *Schupfnudeln* below.

Reibekuchen or **Reiberdatschi:** see *Kartoffelpuffer* above.

Rinderrouladen: beef roulades are a favorite dish amongst the Germans, and there are innumerable ways of preparing them. The classic filling consists of bacon, onion and pickled gherkins.

Rinderzunge: ox-tongue is highly prized for its tenderness. It is prepared in various ways according to local traditions. It may be eaten boiled with a mushroom sauce, broiled and with a crunchy herb topping.

Rollmops mit Kartoffelsalat: rollmops. The herring fillets are covered in mustard, stuffed with onions and gherkins then rolled and marinaded in aromatic vinegar. Eaten cold as appetizers or as a light dinner with potato salad.

Rote-Bete-Salat or **Rote-Rüben:** a side dish consisting of boiled beetroot salad, often seasoned with oil, vinegar and finely chopped raw onion.

Rotkohl or **Blaukraut (mit Äpfeln):** red cabbage is eaten in every region of Germany, but is best-loved with a good crisp roast duck, goose or pork. It is normally prepared with bay leaves and cloves or in a sweet-and-sour sauce with wine, vinegar, sugar, onion and pieces of apple. Try it!

Rumpsteak: grilled rump steak, served with French fries. A dish imported from America but adopted as a classic of German cuisine.

Sahnehering mit Salzkartoffeln: herring fillets in a cream-based sauce with onions and gherkins. Served cold with hot boiled potatoes.

Sauerampfersuppe: sorrel soup. This appetizer is made with potato and this rather pungent herb, seasoned with pepper and nutmeg.

Sauerbraten: originally from the Rhineland, this 'sour' roast is one of the most popular German dishes. Beef is left to marinade for three or four days in vinegar and wine, after which it is roasted in the oven. In the Rhineland the juices are sweetened with raisins and walnuts. In Bavaria the sauce is made with lemon and soured cream. In other areas there are still more variations. The meat is served with *Knödel* (see above) and red cabbage, or perhaps with apple or blueberry sauce.

Sauerkraut: found throughout Germany. Shredded white cabbage is salted to produce the milky acid that gives this dish its particular flavour, and makes it more digestible. Often boiled in wine with bay leaves and cumin and served with meat or sausages.

Saure Klopse: see *Königsberger Klopse* above.

Saure Kutteln: tripe boiled in white wine and vinegar is hardly found at all in northern Germany, while it is very popular in the south. Eaten with a bread roll, as an appetizer.

Schaschlik(spieß) mit Pommes frites: a skewer of meat and, sometimes, vegetables such as bell peppers, in a spicy sauce, served with French fries. One of the classics offered by the *Imbiß* (see 'Where to Eat').

Schinken im Brotteig: a recipe that came originally from Eastern Europe. A whole joint of ham is covered in puff pastry and then baked in the oven. Served carved into slices.

Schinkennudeln: boiled noodles, fried in a pan with ham and onion.

Schlachtplatte: a dish of various cold cuts and boiled meats, often served with sauerkraut and (perhaps mashed) potatoes.

Schlesische Häckerle: salted herrings, hard-boiled eggs, bacon, gherkins and onion mixed together, chopped up and spread on wholemeal bread. Can be served as a main course with potatoes boiled in their skins.

Schnitzel Holstein: this dish does not take its name from the place, but from a politician at the time of Bismarck. Fried veal escalopes in breadcrumbs topped with fried eggs and anchovies and capers. Served with a slice of white bread covered with sardines in oil, smoked salmon and caviar.

Schupfnudeln: potato dumplings. Found only in southern Germany, they are known locally by various names: *Bauchstecherla, Bubespitzle, Buwespitz, Fingernudeln, Ranzenstecher.*

Seezunge Müllerinart: sole in breadcrumbs, fried in butter and served with melted butter.

Selleriesalat: a traditional German side dish, made with cold boiled celeriac root. Also eaten raw, chopped very finely with various dressings: oil, vinegar and spices; cream and soured cream; or yoghurt, lemon and spices. Goes extremely well with roast duck or goose.

Spargel mit Höllandischer Soße: (white!) asparagus, normally eaten with Hollandaise sauce and boiled potatoes.

Spargelcremesuppe: cream of asparagus soup.

Spargelröllchen: served as an appetizer or part of a cold buffet. Asparagus in mayonnaise rolled in slices of cold ham.

Strammer Max: a slice of cold cut meat or ham and a fried egg on a piece of bread. Eaten as a snack or quick dinner.

Tomatencremesuppe: cream of tomato soup.

Ziguenerschnitzel: veal escalope in tomato and paprika sauce. Usually rather spicy. Also known as *Paprikaschnitzel.* Often served with French fries and salad.

Zwiebelkuchen: a type of quiche usually prepared in regions which produce *Federweißer* wine (young wine, see 'Drinks'). A pastry base filled with onions and smoked bacon.

Zwiebelsuppe: a winter appetizer which originated in France (in fact, it is often known as *Französische Zwiebelsuppe*). It consists of a broth with lots of chopped onions which is placed in the oven covered with a slice of cheese. Beware: underneath the cheese, the soup stays boiling hot. Because the heat and the onions make one sweat, it is a very effective remedy in the early stages of a cold.

SWITZERLAND

It is very difficult to draw up a list of national Swiss dishes, as each valley preserves its own culinary traditions and customs. Also, the cuisine of each canton reflects that of the neighboring country (Italy, France, Germany, Austria). Therefore the following list contains only the most famous of dishes from German-speaking Switzerland, each of which will be found in the big cities. In areas less frequented by tourists, allow the waiter to recommend a local speciality.

Basler Lummelbraten: fillet of beef roasted with smoked bacon and served with fresh vegetables.

Berner Ratsherrenplatte: a mixed plate of fillets and other cuts of roast meat, served with *Rösti* (see below).

Berner Rösti: a mixed grill, sometimes served on a bed of sauerkraut.

Bircher Müsli: famous the world over as a healthy breakfast, original Swiss muesli is a mixture of oat flakes, chopped walnuts and fresh fruit (or dried fruit if the latter is unavailable). Eaten with milk or yoghurt, usually at breakfast.

Bündner Fleisch: an appetizer consisting of dried and thinly sliced pieces of leg of beef.

Bündner Gerstensuppe: a vegetable soup containing barley and *Bündner Fleisch* (see above).

Cordon bleu: thick veal steaks in breadcrumbs, filled with cheese and ham. Fried and served with boiled potatoes and vegetables.

Fondue bourguignonne: a meat fondue. Similar in concept to the traditional Swiss cheese fondue (see *Fondue neuchâteloise* below). With a meat fondue, however, the meat is cut into small cubes and cooked by each diner at the table in a pot of hot oil. The meat is served with various sauces (both hot and cold), pickles and bread.

Fondue neuchâteloise: the original cheese fondue. Cubes of bread are skewered onto long-handled forks and dipped into the pot containing melted cheese flavored with white wine, kirsch, salt, pepper and nutmeg.

NATIONAL DISHES

Forellen mit Mandeln: fried trout in breadcrumbs, sprinkled with toasted almonds and red wine sauce. Served with white bread and salad.

Geschnetzeltes Kalbfleisch: fillet of beef stewed in a thick sauce with cream and mushroom. Served with noodles and salad or, particularly in Zurich, with apple sauce.

Käsefondue: see *Fondue neuchâteloise* above.

Käseschnitte Oberländer Art: butter and mustard spread on a slice of toasted bread, covered with a slice of ham and Emmental cheese, cooked in the oven until the cheese melts. Sometimes served with a fried egg.

Käsewähe: a savory cheese tart.

Raclette: a mature *Raclette* cheese is cut in two and placed in front of the fire until it begins to melt, when it is served with boiled potatoes and pickles. Nowadays there are little electric hot plates which can be used at the table so each guest can prepare their own dish and eat it straight away.

Ratsherrentopf: various fillets of meat with kidneys and calves' liver. Served with peas, carrots and potatoes.

Rösti: thin strips of potato, pan-fried without being stirred, giving an omelet-like dish. Served with fried onions and strips of browned bacon.

Salm nach Basler Art: a slice of salmon, fried in butter with lots of onion.

Schwyzer Käsesuppe: a traditional Swiss peasant dish. A kind of pudding made with fresh homemade bread and Alpine cheese.

Zuger Rötel: salmon trout cooked in white wine, cream and herbs. Eaten in the winter months.

Zürcher Leberspießli: skewers of calves' liver fried with smoked bacon and sage. Served with string beans and boiled potatoes.

Züri Gschnätzlets: thinly cut slices of various meats, calves' liver and mushrooms and cream. Served with the inevitable *Rösti*.

REGIONAL DISHES

Given the relative homogeneity of Austrian and Swiss
gastronomic culture, not to mention the difference in size of
the countries concerned, we have chosen to explore in detail,
i.e. region by region, only the specialities of Germany. In
eastern parts of Germany there are enormous poultry farms,
while in the Rhineland potatoes and cabbages are found in
every shape and color imaginable. However, it can be said
that traditionally meat is the favorite food throughout the
country, even if today one can find imaginative vegetarian
dishes, particularly in places frequented by a younger
clientele.

HAMBURG

Fischpastete: puff pastry filled with various kinds of fish and
asparagus, or other vegetables, and cream.

Fliederbeersuppe mit Schneeklößchen: a unique appetizer,
which takes the form of a hot, sweet soup of elderberries,
pears and plums cooked in red wine and bound with starch,
with clouds of whipped egg white and sugar floating on top.
In summer it may also be served cold.

Grüner Aal: eel cooked in wine and stock, served with
bechamel sauce or melted butter and boiled potatoes.

Hamburger Fischsuppe: a fish soup made with fish fresh from
the North Sea.

Kabeljau nach Hamburger Art: cod cooked in white wine
and served in oyster sauce.

REGIONAL DISHES

Labskaus: a typical sailors' dish, invented many years ago by a ship's cook. It is jokingly said that whatever has been lost during the year will turn up in this dish. Fortunately nowadays the freshest ingredients are used to make more delicate versions. The usual ingredients are pickled herring fillets, beetroot, gherkins, beef and potatoes.

Matjesfilet mit Bohnen und Speckkrusteln: the pickled herring fillets are served cold and make an interesting contrast to the hot string beans and pieces of crispy bacon.

Schollenfillets auf Finkenwerder Art: the month of May is the best time of year to eat plaice, which are at their best when sprinkled with diced bacon and strips of zucchini.

Vierländer Poularde: chicken fried in butter.

HESSEN

Äbbelwoisuppe: a soup made with *Äbbelwoi* (see 'Drinks'), the wine produced from apple juice.

Frankfurter Platte: a mixed selection of sausages and sauerkraut.

Gänsebrust in der Salzkruste: goose breasts, rolled in slices of bacon, and baked under a layer of beaten egg white, coarse salt and flour. The salt crust and bacon are removed before serving. This way of cooking prevents the meat from drying out and preserves it flavour.

REGIONAL DISHES

Geröstel: a selection of various sausages, pig's liver and pig's head, all cut up into cubes and pan-fried together with onions, potatoes and gherkins. Halfway through the cooking process eggs are added. When the eggs are set, the dish is served with *Krautsalat*, the white cabbage and cumin salad.

Handkäse mit Musik: a cheese (see also 'Cheeses') marinated in vinegar, oil, onion and pepper. Served as an appetizer or a snack.

Ochsenschwanzragout: a meat sauce made with oxtail.

Rinderbrust mit Grüner Soße: boiled brisket of beef, served with the local speciality: green sauce, known as *Gri Soos* in the local dialect. It is made with yoghurt, cream, lemon and herbs, and every family has its own secret recipe.

Zwiebel gefüllt: large mild onions are hollowed out, stuffed with ground meat, stale bread and various spices, and baked in the oven, sometimes on a bed of salt to give them more flavor.

BADEN-WÜRTTEMBERG

Brotsuppe: pieces of bread and browned onion are soaked in a mixture of meat stock, water and milk. In olden times this was eaten at breakfast in the countryside.

Gaisburger Marsch: an *Eintopf* (see 'Gastronomic Terms') made with meat stock, potatoes, *Spätzle* (see below) and pieces of boiled meat, served with browned onions.

Hasenterrine or **Hasenkuchen:** a rather unusual soufflé made with ground hare meat and fillet of hare, with slices of bacon, prunes and pistacchio nuts. Can be eaten hot, but when it has been chilled overnight the fine gamey flavors are really at their best.

Hirnsuppe: brain soup.

Knöpfle: a pasta similar to the *Spätzle* (see below), but somewhat harder.

Kratzete: pieces of broken omelet, the traditional accompaniment to asparagus and ham. Pieces of omelet can also be eaten sprinkled with sugar and cinnamon, as a dessert (similar to the Austrian *Kaiserschmarrn* see 'Desserts').

Laubfrösche: not frogs, as the name suggests, but spinach or chard leaves stuffed with a paste of ground meat, stale bread, eggs and spices.

Linsen auf Schwäbische Art: lentil stew containing pieces of meat, smoked bacon and onion, served with sausages and *Spätzle.*

Maultaschen: ravioli, filled and served in a variety of ways.

Metzelsuppe: not in fact a soup, but a mixture of liver sausage, black pudding and boiled bacon. This used to eaten to celebrate the slaughter of the animals for meat.

Rehrücken in Rotweinsauce: often known as *Rehrücken Baden-Baden*, even though it did not originate in that city. Roast saddle of venison, covered with pears stuffed with blueberries.

Rehrücken Schwarzwälder Art: marinaded saddle of venison served in a brandy, soured cream and blueberry sauce.

Schneckensuppe: snail soup was once a very ordinary dish, for great quantities of snails could be found in the vineyards. They are cooked in a veal stock with a little dry white wine and seasoned with salt, pepper, chilli pepper, garlic and various herbs. The soup is thickened with cream.

Spätzle: the side dish *par excellence*. Homemade short egg pasta, boiled in stock. Variants include: *Spinatspätzle* (with spinach); *Käsespätzle* (placed in a roasting tin with Swiss cheese and golden onion rings), *Steinpilzspätzle* (with porcini mushrooms).

Speckkuchen: a savory flan with bacon (see also *Zwiebelkuchen* under 'National Dishes').

Zwetschgensuppe: a cold soup made from puréed plums and wine and cinammon. Eaten as an appetizer in the summer, as well as as a dessert.

LOWER SAXONY

Aalsuppe: eel and vegetable soup. Sometimes just the broth is served, sometimes *Knödel* are added.

Heidelammkeule geschmort: on the moors around Lüneburg lives a little-known breed of sheep, whose meat has an intense, almost gamey flavor, and is much in demand amongst gourmets. For this dish the meat is stewed in wine with rosemary, garlic, potatoes, zucchini and bell peppers.

Lammhaxen auf Bohnpüree: shank of lamb boiled in vegetable stock with herbs. Served on mashed beans.

Zander mit Meerrettichkruste: the *Zander* is a freshwater fish of the perch family. It is covered with butter, horseradish, apple and spices and baked in the oven. The apple tempers the strong flavor of the horseradish.

BAVARIA

Biersuppe: only the Bavarians could have invented beer soup! It is made with flour or corn starch, sugar, egg, cloves, cinnamon and as much beer as it takes to mix the ingredients together.

Blaue Zipfel: pieces of Nuremburg sausages boiled in a sauce of vinegar, onion and spices. Cooking the sausages in vinegar gives them the blueish color which gives the dish its name. Served with horseradish, mustard and homemade bread.

Böfflamott: inherited from the French occupation, this is *Boeuf à la mode*, 'translated' into Bavarian. Beef is marinaded for two or three days in red wine and spices and then cooked in the same juices.

Fränkischer Krautbraten: a white-cabbage stew with ground meat and onion, flavoured with soured cream and bacon.

G'scheltes: smoked bacon or ham cooked with sauerkraut.

Hechtenkraut: pieces of pike, cooked in the oven with sauerkraut and cream.

Kalbshaxe: veal shanks cooked in the oven or on the broiler (see *Schweinshaxe* below).

Kartoffelstrudel: a savory strudel filled with bacon, onion and potatoes.

Leberkäs: a hotchpotch of beef, pork and entrails of both, cooked in the oven with sweet marjoram, nutmeg and other spices. Served hot or cold.

Leberknödel: *Knödel* made with liver, stale bread or potatoes, cooked in the oven and served with sauerkraut.

Leberknödelsuppe: liver *Knödel* soup.

Leber- und Nierenpfanne: offal is a very important ingredient in Bavarian cooking. Unfortunately it has been suggested that nowadays it can contain heavy metals, so offal from young animals is preferred. Occasionally one can treat oneself to a mixed dish of calves' liver and kidney pan-fried with onions and potatoes.

Lüngerl, sauer: calves' lungs are traditionally eaten at about 11 o'clock on Sunday morning, after church, with *Semmelknödel* and a glass of beer.

Markklößchensuppe: marrowballs in a simple broth.

Obazda: flat cheese, usually Camembert, with chopped onion, pepper, salt, chilli pepper, cumin, egg yolk and butter.

Ochsenmaulsalat: a salad made with pieces of ox head in brine, boiled and dressed with a sharp green sauce.

Pichelsteiner Topf: this term covers a range of soups or *Eintopf* . The basic standard is the presence of three types of meat, a variety of vegetables and potatoes.

Schweinshaxe: shank of pork cooked in the oven or on the broiler. The outside must be crisp, while the meat inside must be tender and juicy. In winter it is eaten with *Semmelknödel* (see below) and sauerkraut, or red cabbage; in summer with salad. Whatever the season it is well complemented by a glass of cool beer.

Semmelknödel: *Knödel* made with stale bread, served as a side dish or in soup.

Weißwürste: white sausages made with ground veal, bacon and parsley. Eaten with sweet mustard (*Süßer Senf*) and *Brezel* (see page 6). It is said that 'they must not hear the bells chime midday', i.e. they must only be eaten in the morning. Normally the skin is not eaten, and the meat is sucked out of the sausage in a rather inelegant fashion. Watch a true Bavarian to see how it's done properly!

Wurstsalat: a salad comprising pieces of ham sausage, raw onion rings, vinegar, oil and pepper.

REGIONAL DISHES

BERLIN

Currywurst mit Pommes frites: a fast food dish eaten at the *Imbiß* (see 'Where To Eat') at any time of the day. It is a fried sausage in curried tomato sauce with French fries.

Entenkeulen mit Teltower Rübchen: ducks' thighs with 'Teltower turnips', a Berlin specialty made with a variety of small turnip, which was a favorite of Goethe's. The thighs are cooked in red wine and served with the boiled turnips, a mixture of onion and boiled carrots, and gravy.

Kalbsleber Berliner Art: grilled veal liver covered with slices of apple and golden rings of onion. One of the capital's most famous dishes.

Karpfen mit Buttersauce: carp is traditionally eaten on New Year's Eve, and if you put one of its scales in your wallet, you will never run out of money. Young carp (up to about 2kg) gives the best flavor. Ovencooked in wine and served with new potatoes and salad, it is delicious.

MECKLENBURG-VORPOMMERN

Dorsch gespickt: along the Baltic seaboard young cod is known as *Dorsch*. For this recipe it is larded with (unsmoked) bacon and baked on a bed of vegetables.

Gänsehals: this dish consists of the neck of a goose stuffed with goose liver, pork, smoked bacon, truffle and almonds, fried and served cold or hot with vegetables.

REGIONAL DISHES

Gänseschenkel in Schmorkohl: braised goose thighs with onion and white cabbage, seasoned with sugar and vinegar.

Kabeljau in Senfsauce: boiled cod with a mustard sauce - this recipe has been eaten for generations along the German coast.

Mecklenburger Rippenbraten: roast pork with apple, raisin and prune stuffing.

Rindfleisch mit Pflaumen: a very tasty regional dish. A large piece of beef with prunes and boiled potatoes. Often pieces of browned onion are placed on the meat.

Wildente gebraten mit Zitronensauce: the name suggests a modern creation, but in fact since the end of the nineteenth century wild duck has been served with a lemon sauce to temper its strong flavor.

PALATINATE

Oberfälzer Krengemüse: vegetables (*Gemüse*) are only found in the name of the dish which in fact contains stale bread cooked in stock with egg yolks and flavored with horseradish, saffron, salt and sugar. Eaten as a side dish to accompany *Tellerfleisch* (see 'National Dishes').

Radieschenquark mit Kümmelkartoffeln: this dish is based around low-fat cottage cheese which is mixed with other, more strongly-flavored cheeses, chopped radishes and onion, all of which is garnished with chives and other herbs.

REGIONAL DISHES

Rebhuhn im Weinblatt: partridges rolled in slices of smoked bacon and large vine leaves, and roasted in the oven. Towards the end of the cooking time grapes (with the pips removed) are added to the sauce. The partridges are served with the cooked grapes and a gravy using the cooking juices, white wine and juniper berries.

Rieslinghuhn: chicken roasted in dry white wine (Riesling) and herbs.

Saumagen: this dish frequently appears at state banquets hosted by Chancellor Helmut Kohl for visiting foreign dignitaries, and thus it has become famous throughout the world. The pig's intestine is stuffed with ground meat and broad beans, and cooked in the oven. It is accompanied by a good local wine such as Kallstadter Saumagen, which bears the same name as the dish, or by grape must, known in this region as *Bitzler* (see 'Drinks').

Weinsuppe: wherever good wine is produced one is bound to find a recipe for wine soup. Sometimes raisins, chestnuts, and/or croutons are added. However it is made there is one golden rule: the better the wine, the better the soup.

RHINELAND-WESTPHALIA

Apfel-Blutwurst-Küchlein: when someone from Cologne talks about **Kaviar** (lit. 'caviar') they may mean this dish which consists of *Blutwurst* (see 'Sausages and Cold Cuts') fried with diced onion, apple and potato.

Dicke Bohnen mit Rauchfleisch: a dish similar to *Eintopf* (see 'Gastronomic Terms') made with broad beans, smoked bacon and smoked pork.

Flönz mit Ölk: a *Blutwurst* (see 'Sausages and Cold Cuts') with onion, spread on a rye bread roll.

Halve Hahn (Halber Hahn): not, as you might expect, half a chicken; this is in fact a cheese roll.

Himmel und Erde: this dish is called 'Heaven and Earth' because of its main ingredients. The apples grow beneath the heavens, the potatoes beneath the earth. Pieces of hot sugared apple are covered with a potato purée, and sprinkled with bits of crispy bacon. Sometimes it is served with a slice of pan-fried *Blatwurst* (see 'Sausages and Cold Cuts').

Kalbsnieren in Senfsoße: in the past kidneys were a popular and economical dish. According to this traditional recipe, they are finely sliced and cooked in a mustard sauce.

Muscheln in Weißweinsud: North Sea mussels are found from September/October to March/April. The most enthusiastic consumers of mussels are the people of Rhineland, who most enjoy them cooked in white wine and served with buttered wholemeal bread.

Pfefferpotthast: a spicy beef sauce, known in the city of Dortmund as long ago as 1378. It is served with a thirst-quenching glass of cool beer, such as *Dortmunder Alt* (see 'Drinks').

REGIONAL DISHES

Pillekuchen: see *Schnibbelkuchen* below.

Schnibbelbohnen mit Gehacktem: boiled green beans, sliced and refried with chopped meat. Served with boiled potatoes.

Schnibbelkuchen or **Pillekuchen:** similar to *Kartoffelpuffer* (see 'National Dishes'), but as big as the pan will allow. The raw potatoes are cut into strips or coarsely grated, and pan-fried with onion, salt and pepper. Eaten with wholemeal bread, butter and *Rübenkraut* (see 'Gastronomic Terms').

Stielmus in Sahnsauce: this type of vegetable is hardly known beyond the Rhine valley, where turnips are planted so close together that their roots have no room to develop and only their leaves can grow. According to this recipe the leaves are served in a cream sauce with chunks of tomato.

SAARLAND

Brieswürfel, ausgebacken: the proximity of France is often seen in the cuisine of this region. In this case the veal sweetbread is diced, coated in batter and fried.

Hähnchenkeulen in körniger Senfsauce: chicken thighs cooked in chicken stock, cream, hot mustard, onion, salt and pepper.

Kartoffelscheiben überbacken: a potato gratin, made with

REGIONAL DISHES

slices of boiled potato covered with creamed potatoes,
horseradish and leek.

Maronen: in the wine-producing areas, the climate tends to
be ideal for chestnuts, which go very well with game.
However, the best way to eat them is to nibble on hot
chestnuts with a glass of *Federweißer* (wine still in the process
of fermentation, see 'Drinks').

SAXONY

Frischlingskeulen in der Salzkruste: leg of baby boar covered
with juniper berries and strips of bacon, baked in the oven in
a crust of beaten egg white, coarse salt and flour. After
cooking, the crust is broken and the meat is served in a gravy
made with the cooking juices and cranberry.

Leipziger Allerlei: this means literally 'Leipzig mixture' and
refers to a soup or *Eintopf* made with tasty vegetables (e.g.
asparagus) and sometimes enriched with prawns or highly-
flavored mushrooms.

Schwarzwurzelgemüse: this Alpine root vegetable is boiled
and served as a side dish.

SCHLESWIG-HOLSTEIN

Ente mit Lübscher Füllung: roast duck is eaten all over
northern Germany. In Lübeck it is stuffed with apple, raisins
and breadcrumbs.

Gröner Heinrich: a soup or *Eintopf* (see 'Gastronomic Terms') made with green beans, potatoes, smoked bacon, cooked together with small unpeeled pears.

Grünkohl mit Kasseler und Pinkel: kale served with smoked pork chops in brine and a particular type of sausage. Eaten with sweetened potatoes browned in the pan.

Kieler Sprotten: smoked sprats (small fish similar to herring) from Kiel.

Lübecker Matrosenfleisch: 'Lübeck sailors' meat' is roast beef, served rare on creamed potatoes and garnished with pieces of ham, gherkins, tomatoes and parsley.

Pfannfisch: a kind of soufflé made with fish, vegetables and potatoes bound together with single cream and cooked in the oven.

Note: all recipes serve four. The country of origin is indicated by the symbol for each country: D = Germany; CH = Switzerland; A = Austria.

BAYERISCHE CREME
Bavarian Custard (D)

Ingredients:

wild berries	8 oz (250 g)
clear gelatine	3 sheets
egg yolks	3
sugar	3oz (70 g)
vanilla essence	2 pods' worth
kirsch	3 tablespoons
whipping cream	½ pint (250 ml)
vanilla sugar	1 tablespoon

Method:

Leave the gelatine to soak in cold water. Put the egg yolks, the sugar and the vanilla essence in a bowl and whisk with an electric whisk until you obtain a pale, foamy cream. Drain the gelatine and dissolve it over a low heat in 1 tablespoon of kirsch and some water in a small pan. Whip the cream. Stir 1-2 tablespoons of cream into the gelatine and add it to the egg mixture. Pour in the rest of the cream and mix carefully. Leave to set in the refrigerator for at least two hours. In the meantime prepare the wild fruits, leaving them to steep in the vanilla sugar and the remainder of the kirsch. To serve, immerse the custard mold briefly in hot water and turn it out onto a serving plate. Decorate with the fruit and serve.

RECIPES

HERINGSSALAT
Herring salad (D)

Ingredients:

salted herrings	2
boiled beetroots	4
boiled potatoes	4
cooking apple	1
small cucumber	1
onion	1
red wine vinegar	3 tablespoons
oil	3 tablespoons
chopped chives	1 tablespoon
chopped parsley	1 tablespoon
salt, pepper, lemon juice to taste	

Method:

Leave the herrings to soak, remove the skin and bones. Take the fillets and cut them into ½inch (1cm) cubes. Peel and cube the apple and cucumber. Peel the beetroot and potatoes and cut them into slices ¼inch (½cm) thick. Arrange the slices in alternate layers on a serving plate, leaving a space in the middle. Peel and chop the onion. Make a sauce with the vinegar, lemon juice, salt, pepper and oil, add the chives, parsley, and chopped onion. Marinade the cubes of herring, apple and cucumber in the sauce for half an hour and then place them in the center of the serving plate. Pour the rest of the sauce over the potatoes and beetroot and serve.

HIMMEL UND ERDE
Heaven and Earth (D)

Ingredients:

cooking apples	14 oz (400 g)
floury potatoes	14 oz (400 g)
smoked bacon, cubed	2½ oz (80 g)
butter	1½ oz (40 g)
milk	4 fl oz (100 ml)
lemon juice	1 tablespoon
sugar	1 pinch
nutmeg, salt, pepper to taste	

Method:

Peel and core the apples, cut into cubes and pour the lemon juice over. Peel the potatoes and boil them. When they are cooked, mash them. Heat the milk with a pinch of nutmeg, add the potatoes, salt and pepper. Keep warm. Heat the butter in a pan and add the apple. Sprinkle with sugar and brown. Fry the cubes of bacon in another pan until they become crispy. When the apples are cooked mix them in with the potato purée, pour the mixture in a bowl and sprinkle the bacon pieces on top.

(Never whisk the purée in a food mixer or electric whisk - it ends up like glue!)

HÜHNERFRIKASSE
Chicken Fricassée (D)

Ingredients:

chicken breasts	4
boiled ox tongue in brine	4 oz (100 g)
fresh field mushrooms	4 oz (100 g)
dried mushrooms, soaked overnight	1 oz (30 g)
vegetables for stock	1 bunch
butter	3oz (70 g)
cream	¼ pint (125 ml)
chicken stock	½ pint (250 ml)
lemon juice, salt, pepper to taste	

Method:

Season the chicken breasts with salt and pepper and brown
them in about 1oz (25g) of butter. Wash the stock vegetables,
chop them and add them to the meat. Add the chicken stock
and drained dried mushrooms and leave to cook for fifteen
minutes. Cut the tongue into cubes, add to the pan and cook
for five minutes. Remove the meat and the mushrooms with a
skimmer and keep warm. Strain the cooking juices, add the
cream and warm through. Season with salt, pepper and
lemon juice, add about ¾oz (20g) of finely shaved butter.
Clean the fresh mushrooms, washing them only if necessary,
and fry them lightly in the remaining butter. Arrange them
with the meat on warm plates and cover with the cooking
gravy. Serve with buttered rice.

KALBSSTEAK CORDON BLEU
Veal Cordon Bleu (CH)

Ingredients:

thin veal escalopes	8
slices of ham	4
slices of Swiss cheese	4
egg	1
lemon	1

salt, pepper, ketchup, flour, breadcrumbs
oil for frying.

Method:

Lightly beat the meat, season with salt and pepper and spread ketchup on one side of each escalope. Roll each piece of ham in a slice of cheese and sandwich between two of the escalopes (with the ketchup on the inside), fixing everything in place with a toothpick.

Flour the meat, dip them in the beaten egg and then in breadcrumbs, and fry them on both sides in boiling oil. Garnish with wedges of lemon and served with boiled potatoes, peas and buttered carrots.

RECICPES

RECIPES

KARTOFFELKLÖSSE - KNÖDEL
Potato knödel (D)

Ingredients:

raw floury potatoes	2lb 10 oz (1.2 kg)
floury potatoes boiled in their skins the day before	14 oz (400 g)
flour	2½ oz (80 g)
smoked bacon	1½ oz (40 g)
butter	¾ oz (20 g)
egg yolks	2
bread roll	1
hot milk	(100 ml)
salt, pepper, nutmeg	

Method:

Cut the bacon and the bread roll into pieces. Fry the bacon in a pan until it becomes transparent. Take the pieces of bread and brown them in the butter too. Put to one side. Peel the boiled potatoes and mash them. Peel the raw potatoes, dry them and grate them. Put the grated potatoes in a bowl and pour the milk over. Add the mashed potatoes, the egg yolks, the flour and work the dough with your hands until it becomes smooth. If necessary, drain off any excess water. Season the dough with salt, pepper and nutmeg.
Bring a large pan of water to the boil. Shape discs 3inches (7-8cm) thick from the dough and hollow out the middle. Fill the hollow with the bread and bacon mixture, close over and make into a ball. Cook in boiling salted water for about 20 minutes.

KARTOFFELSALAT
Potato salad (D)

Ingredients:

potatoes	2 lb	(1 kg)
ham	5 oz	(150 g)
peas	3½ oz	(100 g)
hard-boiled eggs	4	
small onions	4	
large pickled gherkins	3	
watercress	1 bunch	
egg yolk	1	
hot meat stock	½ pint	(250 ml)
oil	¼ pint	(125 ml)
wine vinegar	6 tablespoons	
chili pepper, salt, pepper to taste		

Method:

Wash the potatoes and boil them for 35-40 minutes. Peel them and slice finely. In the meantime cut the ham, gherkins and hard-boiled eggs into cubes. Boil the peas for a few minutes in salted water and cool them under running water. Clean the onions and slice them finely. Stir 4 tablespoons of vinegar, salt and pepper into the meat stock, and pour it on the salad. Stir and leave to soak for 10 minutes. Prepare a mayonnaise by mixing the egg yolk with the oil, adding the latter drop by drop. Season with salt, chilli and the remaining vinegar and pour it over the salad. Finally, add a little more stock. Serve with chopped watercress.

KOHLROULADEN - KRAUTWICKEL
Cabbage rolls (D)

Ingredients:

ground beef	8 oz	(250 g)
ground veal	8 oz	(250 g)
smoked bacon, cut into cubes	3 ½	(100 g)
eggs	2	
bread rolls	2	
small onions, chopped	2	
Savoy cabbage leaves	12	
meat stock	1 pint	(500 ml)
chopped parsely	2 tablespoons	
majoram	1 tablespoon	
vinegar	1-2 tablespoons	
oil	2 tablespoons	
salt, pepper, chili pepper to taste		

Method:

Scald the cabbage leaves in boiling water, then immerse them in cold water and drain. Place the bread rolls in cold water, squeeze them, then mix them with the ground meat and the onions. Add the eggs and the parsley, season with marjoram, salt, pepper and chilli pepper and work into a dough. Preheat the oven to 290°F (160°C). Open out the cabbage leaves, place some dough in the center, roll the leaf up from the long side and tie with string.

Heat the oil in a skillet and cook the bacon until it becomes transparent. Place it in an ovendish, add the broth and place the cabbage rolls next to each other. Cover and cook in the oven for one hour. Remove the rolls and keep warm. Briefly boil the cooking juices, strain and pour over the rolls.

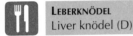

LEBERKNÖDEL
Liver knödel (D)

Ingredients:

calves' liver	8 oz (250 g)
slices of white bread, with crusts removed	3 (c100 g)
eggs	2
butter	¾ oz (20 g)
milk	2-3 tablespoons
marjoram	½ tablespoon
breadcrumbs	2 tablespoons
salt, pepper, nutmeg, oil for frying as necessary	

Method:

Cut one slice of bread into cubes and fry them in the butter. Soak the rest of the bread in the milk and then squeeze it well. Purée the liver. Beat the white of one egg until it becomes stiff. Mix the liver in with the remaining yolk, the other whole egg, the soaked bread and the fried bread. Season with salt, pepper, marjoram, and nutmeg. Leave to stand for at least 30 minutes.

From the dough make small balls. Coat them with the whipped egg white and then the breadcrumbs, ensuring the coating is secure. Fry the balls in boiling oil at 350°F (180°C), then drain. Serve as a main dish, with sauerkraut on the side, or as often found in Germany, in the soup known as *Leberknödelsuppe* (see 'Regional Dishes').

PICHELSTEINER TOPF
Mixed boiled meats (D)

Ingredients:

potatoes	10 ½ oz (300 g)
brisket of beef	8 oz (250 g)
shoulder of pork	8 oz (250 g)
brisket of veal	8 0z (250 g)
beef marrow	2 oz (50 g)
celeriac	½
Savoy cabbage	¼
onions	2
large carrots	2
parsely roots (optional)	2
turnip cabbage	2
bunch of parsley, chopped	1
oil	3 tablespoons
salt, pepper to taste	

Method:

Rinse and dry the meat, and cut into cubes. Cut up the marrow and let it melt in a skillet over a medium heat. Brown the meat in the hot marrow, add 1 liter of water, cover and cook for 20 minutes. In the meantime peel and chop the onions, carrots, celeriac, parsley root (if used), turnip cabbage and potatoes, cutting them into pieces of the same size. Remove the largest leaves from the Savoy cabbage and cut the rest into even pieces. Heat the oil in a large pan and fry the onions. Add the vegetables and brown them for a few minutes. Add the vegetables to the meat, cover and cook for about one hour. Before serving, season to taste and add the chopped parsley.

 ROTE GRÜTZE (D)

Ingredients:

For the berry pudding:

strawberries	8 oz	(250 g)
raspberries	8 oz	(250 g)
blueberries	7 0z	(200 g)
blackberries	7 oz	(200 g)
cherries	7 oz	(200 g)
(any red fruit will do)		
sugar	2 oz	(50 g)
juice of 1 lemon		

For the sauce:

cream	12 fl oz	(300 ml)
sugar	3 tablespoons	
vanilla pod		

Method:

Wash the strawberries and the raspberries, liquidize and strain them. Wash and stone the cherries and add them to the remaining berries. Cover with the lemon juice and the sugar. Leave for a few minutes, then add the liquidised fruit and leave to chill in the refrigerator.

For the sauce: boil 8 fl oz (200ml) of the cream with the open vanilla pod and cook for 4-5 minutes. Remove the vanilla pod and allow the cream to cool, stirring. Whip the remaining cream and add it to the boiled cream. Pour the fruit into small bowls and cover with the cream sauce.

(In the original recipe the fruit purée or redcurrant and raspberry juice is thickened with cornflour or gelatine; however, the flavor of fruit in the version given here is unsurpassable!)

SACHERTORTE (A)

Ingredients:

chocolate	14 oz (400 g)
apricot jam	7 oz (200 g)
sugar	6 oz (160 g)
flour	5½ (140 g)
butter	5½ (140 g)
eggs	8
confectioner's sugar	1 oz (30 g)
powdered yeast	1 teaspoon

Method:

Combine the butter with the sugar, melt half of the chocolate in a bain marie, let it cool while stirring, add it to the butter/sugar mixture and beat until it becomes frothy. One at a time, add the yolks of all the eggs while beating.

Beat the whites of the eggs with the confectioner's sugar until they become stiff, and add them gradually to the chocolate cream. Then, gradually again, add the yeast and the flour. Place the mixture in a cake pan lined with silver foil or greaseproof paper and bake for about 50 minutes at 375° (190°C).

Allow the cake to cool, remove it from the pan, cut it horizontally, spread warmed apricot jam over, and leave a while to absorb. Melt the remaining chocolate in a bain marie and use to ice the cake.

Salzburger Nockerln
Salzburg meringues (A)

Ingredients:

egg whites	*4*
egg yolks	*3*
granulated sugar	*2 oz (50 g)*
butter	*1 ½ (40 g)*
flour	*¾ (20 g)*
a sachet of vanilla sugar	

Method:

Whip the egg whites and add all of the sugar. Remove 3 tablespoons of the whipped egg whites, mix them with the egg yolks and return to the rest of the beaten egg whites. Sieve the flour into the mixture and stir gently. Melt the butter in a shallow baking tray. Using a spoon, make the *Nocklern* (little balls using one spoonful of the mixture each) and place them on the baking tray. Cook them in a hot preheated oven for 8-10 minutes. Serve immediately, protecting them from cold air.

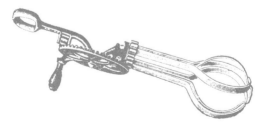

RECIPES

SAUERBRATEN
Sweet-and-sour beef (D)

Ingredients:

fillet of beef	2 lb (1 kg)
fat for frying	2½ (80 g)

For the marinade:

water	1 pint (500 ml)
vinegar	½ pint (250 ml)
salt	1 spoonful
onion	2
carrot	1
peppercorns	5
cloves	2
bay leaf	1
juniper berries	2

For the sauce:

raisins	4 oz (125 g)
peppered breadcrumbs	3 oz (75 g)
soured cream	½ pint (250 ml)
apple sauce or jam	1 tablespoon
salt, pepper	

Method:
Rinse and dry the meat. Bring the the ingredients for the marinade to the boil and leave to cool. Place the meat in an earthenware pot, and pour over the cold marinade. Leave to stand for 2 or 3 days, stirring from time to time. Remove the meat from the marinade and drain. Brown it in the fat and

leave to cook for about 90 minutes. While it is cooking, strain the marinade and keep pouring a little over the meat to prevent it sticking. Add the soaked raisins, and cook them with the meat for 15 minutes. Season the juices with salt and pepper, thicken them with the breadcrumbs and add the apple sauce and the soured cream. Serve with a side dish of *Kartoffelklöße* or *Kartoffelpuffer* (see 'National Dishes').

RECITES

 Sauerkraut (D)

Ingredients:

white cabbage	1½ lb (750 g)
lard	1½ oz (40 g)
apples	2
onion	1
smoked bacon	1 rasher
white wine (e.g. Riesling)	¼ pint (125 ml)
water	¼ pint (125 ml)
chives	1 bunch
bay leaf	1
cumin	½ teaspoon
peppercorns	5
dried juniper berries	3
a pinch of sugar	

Method:

Peel and dice the apples and onion. Heat the lard in a skillet and brown the apple and onions. Sprinkle with a little sugar, add the cabbage and brown it too (do not overwash the cabbage or it will lose its flavor and its vitamin C!). Make the spices into a bouquet garni, and add to the cabbage. Pour on the wine and the water and bring to the boil. Lay the bacon over the cabbage. Cover the pan and leave to cook for 40 minutes on a low heat. Remove the bouquet garni and the bacon and served the cabbage, sprinkled with chives.

SCHWEINSHAXE
Shank of pork (D)

Ingredients:

(rear) shanks of pork	*2 (c. 800 g each)*
stout	*½ pint 250 ml*
onions	*2*
clove of garlic	*1*
cumin	*1 teaspoon*
salt and pepper to taste	

Method:

Score the skin of the meat with diamond patterns. Rinse, dry and season with salt and pepper. Preheat the oven to 320°F (160°C). Peel and finely chop the onions and garlic, add the cumin and place in a skillet with the meat, adding a little water. Cover and cook in the oven for 90 minutes, basting the meat every so often.

Remove the lid, raise the temperature of the oven to 390° (200°C) and cook for a further 30 minutes, until the shanks are brown and crispy on the outside, occasionally pouring a little beer over the meat. Remove the shanks and leave to stand. Liquidize and filter the cooking juices, and return to the heat. If necessary add a little more beer. Remove the meat from the bone and serve it with the gravy, *Knödel* (see above) and red cabbage.

ALPHABET

The German alphabet is the same as in English, but you will find Umlaut: ä, ö and ü. The symbol ß, represents the sound of two 's's or an 's' and 'z' together. The following list gives the pronunciation for each letter, and the phonetic word used in spelling. (see also 'Pronunciation')

A	wie	**Anton**	**N**		**Nordpol**
ah	*vee*	*anton*	*èn*		*nortpol*
B	for	**Berta**	**O**		**Otto**
bay		*bèrta*	*oh*		*otto*
C		**Cäsar**	**P**		**Paula**
tsay		*tsaysar*	*pay*		*powla*
D		**Dora**	**Q**		**Quelle**
day		*dora*	*koo*		*kvèlle*
E		**Emil**	**R**		**Richard**
ay		*aymeel*	*ayr*		*rish-hart*
F		**Friedrich**	**S**		**Siegfried**
èf		*freedrish*	*ès*		*zeeg-freed*
G		**Gustav**	**T**		**Theodor**
gay		*goostaf*	*tay*		*tayo-dor*
H		**Heinrich**	**U**		**Ulrich**
hàh		*highnrish*	*oo*		*ool-rish*
I		**Ida**	**V**		**Viktor**
ee		*eeda*	*fow*		*viktor*
J		**Julius**	**W**		**Wilhelm**
yot		*yoo-lee-oos*	*vay*		*vil-helm*
K		**Konrad**	**X**		**Xanten**
ka		*konrat*	*ix*		*ksanten*
L		**Ludwig**	**Y**		**Ypsilon**
èl		*loodvikh*	*ipsilon*		*oopsilon*
M		**Martin**	**Z**		**Zeppelin**
èm		*martin*	*tsèt*		*tseppeleen*

Things to remember

In the Konditoreien *(cakeshops)* you will find an infinite variety of sweets, cakes and pastries. There will often be a **Café** inside the shopping malls where you can sit with a cup of coffee or a hot chocolate and try the tempting cakes displayed there.

What are these?	**Was ist das?** *vas ist das*
What's in this cake?	**Was ist in dieser Torte?** *vas ist in deeser torte*
I'd like a small/ medium tray of pastries.	**Ich hätte gern ein kleines/ mittelgroßes Tablett mit Gebäck.** *ish hètte gern ine klighnes/mittel- grosses tablèt mit gebèk*
I'd like an assortment of pastries.	**Ich hätte gern eine Auswahl an Teilchen.** *ich hètte gèrn ighne owsvaal an tighlchen*
How much does it/ do they cost?	**Was kostet das/kosten die?** *vas kostet das/kosten dee*
Is there chocolate in those pastries?	**Ist in diesen Teilchen Schokolade?** *ist in deesen tighlshen shokolade*
I would like a slice of that chocolate/ fruit cake/with cream.	**Ich hätte gerne ein Stück von der Schokoladentorte/Obsttorte/mit Sahne** *ish hètte gerne ine shtook fon der shokoladentorte/opsttorte/mit saane*

CHILDREN

Things to remember

The number of 'kinderfreundlich' (children-friendly) restaurants and hotels has increased over recent years, and continues to do so. These places will provide at least a cot, high chair and some kind of game for the youngest members of your family. Most restaurants have children's menus, offering smaller cheaper portions.

I have a small child/ two children.

Ich habe ein kleines Kind/zwei Kinder
ish haabe ine klighnes kint/tsvai kinder

Do you have a special rate for children?

Haben Sie Vergünstigungen für Kinder?
haaben see fergoonstigungen foor kinder

Do you have a cot?

Haben Sie ein Kinderbett?
haaben see ine kinder-bet

Do you have a children's menu?

Haben Sie Kindergerichte?
haaben see kinder-gerishte

Can you warm the baby's bottle?

Können Sie mir das Fläschchen aufwärmen?
kernnen see meer das flèsh-shen aufvèrmen

Where can I feed/ change the baby?

Wo kann ich das Kind stillen/wickeln?
vo kan ish das kint shtillen/vikeln

Do you have a high chair?

Haben Sie einen Kinderstuhl?
haaben see ighnen kinder-shtool

Is there a garden where the children can play?

Gibt es einen Garten, wo die Kinder spielen können?
gipt es ighnen garten, vo dee kinder shpeelen kernnen

Things to remember

Coffee in Germany tends to be a very relaxed affair. You will sit down and take your time over your coffee. Don't be surprised if strangers come and sit at your table, this is quite normal if there are no other places free.

A coffee/a white coffee/ an expresso, please.	**Einen Kaffee/ einen Milchkaffee/ einen Espresso, bitte.** *ighnen kafay, ighnen milsh-kaffay, ighnen èsprèsso, bitte*
A slice of chocolate cake (with cream).	**Ein Stück Schokoladenkuchen (mit Sahne).** *ine shterk shokolaaden-kerkhen (mit sahne)*
A cup of hot chocolate (with cream).	**Eine Tasse heiße Schokolade (mit Sahne).** *ighne tasse haysse shokolaade (mit sahne)*
A draught beer.	**Ein Bier vom Faß.** *ine beer fom fass*
A lager/stout.	**Ein Helles/Dunkles.** *ine helles/doonkles*
A cup of tea with lemon.	**Einen Tee mit Zitrone.** *ighnen tay mit tsitrone*
A glass of mineral water.	**Ein Glas Mineralwasser.** *ine glaas mineral-vasser*

With ice,
please.

Mit Eis, bitte.
mit ighs, bitte

Another cup of
coffee, please.

Noch eine Tasse Kaffee, bitte.
nokh ine tasse kaffay, bitte

We would like an
aperitif.

Wir hätten gern einen Aperitif.
veer hetten gern ighnen aperitif

Waiter!

Kellner! / Herr Ober!
kèllner! hèr ober

Bring me the bill,
please.

Bringen Sie mir bitte die Rechnung.
*bringen see meer bitte dee
reshnungh*

COMPLAINTS

This doesn't work.	**Das funktioniert nicht.** *das funktsioneert nisht*
It's faulty.	**Das ist defekt.** *das ist defekt*
We are still waiting to be served.	**Wir warten noch darauf, bedient zu werden.** *veer varten nokh darowf, bedeent tsoo verden*
The coffee is cold.	**Der Kaffee ist kalt.** *der kaffay ist kalt*
This meat is tough.	**Dieses Fleisch ist zäh.** *deeses flighsh ist zè*
The tablecloth is dirty.	**Das Tischtuch ist nicht sauber.** *das tish-tukh ist nisht sowber*
The room is noisy.	**Das Zimmer ist nicht ruhig.** *das tsimmer ist nisht roohik*
It's too smoky here.	**Hier ist zu viel Rauch.** *heer ist tsoo feel rowch*

CONVERSATION

Things to remember

> Many Germans, Swiss and Austrians speak English and they
> will be happy to try out the conversational skills they acquired
> on holiday or at school. However, don't be shy about trying to
> start a conversation in German.

I'm English.	**Ich bin Engländer/Engländerin** *ish bin englender/englenderin*
I don't speak German.	**Ich spreche kein deutsch.** *ish shpreshe kine doytsh*
What's your name? (formal/informal)	**Wie heißen Sie/heißt Du?** *vee highssen see/highsst doo*
My name is...	**Ich heiße...** *ish highsse*
Do you mind if I sit here?	**Stört es Sie, wenn ich mich hier hinsetze?** *shterrt es see, venn ish mish heer hinsetse*
Is this place free?	**Ist dieser Platz frei?** *ist deeser plats fry*
Where are you from?	**Wo kommen Sie her?** *vo kommen see her*
I am from ...	**Ich komme aus...** *ish komme ows*
Can I offer you a coffee/something to drink?	**Kann ich Sie zu einem Kaffee/etwas zum Trinken einladen?** *kan ish see tsu ighnem kaffay/etvas zoom trinken ighnladen*

Things to remember

The German currency is the mark (DM, divided into 100 Pfennig), in Austria it's the schilling (ÖS, 100 Groschen), in Switzerland the Swiss franc (Sfr, 100 centimes). Take your passport with you when you go to the bank to change your money.

Do you have any change?	**Haben Sie Kleingeld?** *haaben see klighn-gelt*
Can you change a fifty-mark note?	**Können Sie einen Fünfzigmarkschein wechseln?** *kernen see ighnen foonftsig-mark-shighn vèxeln*
I'd like to change these traveller's cheques.	**Ich möchte gern diese Reisechecks einlösen.** *ish mershte gern deese righse-shèx ighnlersen*
I would like to change these pounds into deutschmarks	**Ich möchte gern Pfund in D-Mark wechseln.** *ish mershte gern pfoont in daymark vèxeln*
What is the rate for dollars?	**Wie steht der Kurs für den Dollar?** *vee shtayt der koors foor dayn dollar*
Can I withdraw cash with my credit card.	**Kann ich auf meine Kreditkarte Bargeld bekommen?** *kan ish owf mine kredeet-karte bargelt bekommen*
I would like to transfer funds from my account.	**Ich möchte gern Geld von meinem Konto überweisen.** *ish mershte gern gelt fon mighnem konto oobervighsen*

DATES AND CALENDAR

| What is the date today? | **Welches Datum ist heute?** |
| | *velshes datum ist hoyte* |

| First of March | **der erste März** |
| | *der erste mèrz* |

| Second of June | **der zweite Juni** |
| | *der zvighte yoonee* |

| We will be arriving on the 27th of June. | **Wir kommen am 27. Juni an.** |
| | *veer kommen am seeben-oont-tsvantsigsten yoonee an* |

| 1999 | **Neunzehnhundertneunundneunzig** |
| | *noyntsayn-hoondert-noyn-oont-noyn-tsik* |

Monday	**Montag**	*montak*
Tuesday	**Dienstag**	*deenstak*
Wednesday	**Mittwoch**	*mitvokh*
Thursday	**Donnerstag**	*donnerstak*
Friday	**Freitag**	*frightak*
Saturday	**Samstag**	*samstak*
Sunday	**Sonntag**	*sontak*

January	**Januar**	*yannooar*
February	**Februar**	*faybrooar*
March	**März**	*mèrz*
April	**April**	*april*
May	**Mai**	*migh*
June	**Juni**	*yoonee*
July	**Juli**	*yuulee*
August	**August**	*owgoost*
September	**September**	*september*
October	**Oktober**	*oktober*
November	**November**	*november*
December	**Dezember**	*daytsember*

DIRECTIONS

Excuse me, where is the station?	**Entschuldigung, wo ist der Bahnhof?** *ent-shooldigoong, vo ist der baanhof*
How do I get to the airport?	**Wie komme ich zum Flughafen?** *vee komme ish zoom flook-haafen*
Could you show me the way to the station?	**Können Sie mir die Straße zum Bahnhof zeigen?** *kernnen see meer dee shtraasse zoom baanhof zighgen*
Is this the road that leads to the cathedral?	**Ist das die Straße zum Dom?** *ist das dee shtraasse zoom dom*
I'm looking for the tourist information office.	**Ich suche das Touristen-Informationsbüro.** *ich sukhe das tureesten-informatsions-booro*
Which road do I take for ...?	**Welche Straße muß ich nach ... nehmen?** *velshe shtraasse mooss ish nakh ... naymen*
How long does it take to get there?	**Wie lange braucht man dorthin?** *vee lange browkht man dortheen*
Excuse me, can you tell me where the ... restaurant is?	**Entschuldigung, können Sie mir sagen, wo das Restaurant ... ist?** *ent-shooldigoong, kernnen see meer sagen, vo das restorong ... ist*

EATING OUT 1

Things to remember

> Even in mid-quality restaurants, as well as in pubs and cafés,
> strangers may sit down at your table, if no other places free.
> This might seem strange to you at first, but it doesn't mean you
> are expected to strike up a conversation with them. They will
> often sit back to back with you, and they will probably take no
> notice of you at all. Some restaurants must be booked...

Good evening, we would like a table for two?	**Guten Abend, wir hätten gern einen Tisch für zwei Personen.** *gooten aabent, veer hètten geèrn ighnen tìsh foor tsvigh personen.*
We would like a table in a quiet corner.	**Wir hätten gern einen Tisch in einer ruhigen Ecke.** *veer hètten gern ighnen tish in ighner roohigen ekke*
We have booked a table for two, in the name of ...	**Wir haben einen Tisch für zwei Personen vorbestellt, auf den Namen ...** *veer haben ighnen tìsh foor tsvigh personen vor-bestellt, owf den naamen ...*
Can we eat outside?	**Kann man draußen essen?** *kan man drowssen essen*
We would like a table away from/ near the window.	**Wir hätten gern einen Tisch nicht am Fenster/ am Fenster.** *veer hètten gern ighnen tìsh nisht am fenster/ am fenster*

Is there an entrance for the disabled?	**Gibt es einen Eingang für Behinderte?** *gipt es ighnen ighngang foor behinderte*
Do you speak English?	**Sprechen Sie Englisch?** *shprekhen see english*
Is there a fixed-price menu?	**Haben Sie ein Menü zum Festpreis.** *haben see ine maynoo zoom fest-prighs*
Can we see the menu?	**Können wir die Speisekarte haben?** *kernnen veer dee shpighse-karte haben*
Is there a vegetarian dish?	**Haben Sie ein vegetarisches Gericht?** *haben see ine vegaytarishes gerisht*
What is the specialty of the house?	**Was ist die Spezialität des Hauses?** *vas ist dee shpetseealitèèt des howses*
What is the dish of the day?	**Was ist das Tagesgericht?** *vas ist das taages-gerisht*
What do you recommend?	**Was können Sie uns empfehlen?** *vas kernnen see oons empfaylen*
What's in this dish?	**Woraus besteht dieses Gericht?** *vorows beshtayt deeses gerisht*
Is it spicy?	**Ist das scharf?** *ist das shaarf*

EATING OUT 3

I'm allergic to
bell peppers.

Ich bin gegen Paprika allergisch.
ish bin gaygen papreeka allèrgish

Is there garlic/pepper
in this dish?

**Enthält dieses Gericht
Knoblauch/Pfeffer?**
*entèlt deeses gerisht
knoblowkh/pfèffer*

Could you bring me
the salt/pepper.

Bringen Sie mir bitte Salz/Pfeffer.
bringen see meer bitte salts/pfèffer

Four coffees, please.

Vier Kaffee, bitte.
feer kàffay, bitte

Do you have ...?

Haben Sie ...?
haaben see ...

I'd/We'd like ...

Ich hätte/wir hätten gern ...
ish hètte/veer hètten gern ...

Can you bring me/
us...

Bringen Sie mir/uns ...
bringen see meer/oons ...

I'd like a portion/
half a portion of ...

**Ich hätte gern eine Portion/eine
halbe Portion ...**
*ish hètte gern ighne portsion/ighne
halbe portsion ...*

I'd like to taste ...

Ich möchte ... probieren.
ish mershte ... probeeren

Can you bring us
some bread, please?

Wir hätten gern etwas Brot.
veer hètten gern etvas brot

What are the typical local dishes?

Welche Gerichte sind typisch für diese Gegend?
velshe gerishte sint toopish foor deese gaygent

What is the typical local cheese?

Welcher Käse ist typisch für diese Gegend?
velsher kayse ist toopish foor deese gaygent

What dessert/fruit do you have?

Welche Nachspeisen/welches Obst haben Sie?
velshe nakh-shpaysen/velches opst haben see

We would like a portion of ... with two plates.

Wir hätten gern eine Portion ... mit zwei Tellern.
veer hètten gern ighne portsion ... mit tsvigh tellern

Bring me the bill, please.

Bringen Sie mir bitte die Rechnung.
bringen see meer bitte dee reshnoong

Waiter!

Herr Ober! Kellner!
hèr ober! kèllner!

Will we have to wait long?

Müssen wir lange warten?
moossen veer lange varten

Where is the coatcheck?

Wo ist die Garderobe?
vo ist dee garderobe

Is there a coatstand?

Haben Sie einen Kleiderständer?
haben see ighnen klighder-shtènder

Could you turn the fan/the heating on?

Könnten Sie den Ventilator/die Heizung einschalten?
kernten see den venti-lator/dee hightsoong ighnshalten

What drinks do you have?

Was haben Sie für Getränke?
vas haben see foor getraynke

What beers do you have?

Welche Biersorten führen Sie?
velshe beer-sorten fooren see

A small caraffe of wine, please.

Einen Viertelliter offenen Wein, bitte.
ighnen veertel-leeter offenen vighn, bitte

Where is the buffet for the apetizers?

Wo ist das Vorspeisen-Buffet?
vo ist das vorshpighsen-booffay

Is the fish fresh/frozen?

Ist der Fisch frisch/tiefgekühlt?
ist der fish frish/teefgekoolt

Does this dish come with a side order?

Ist bei diesem Gericht eine Beilage dabei?
ist bigh deesem gerisht ighne bighlage dabigh

Can we have a selection of side dishes?

Könnten wir einen gemischten Beilagenteller haben?
kernten veer ighnen gemishten bighlagen-teller haben

I would like it cooked with little salt.

Ich hätte es gerne salzarm gekocht.
ish hètte es gerne saltsarm gekokht

I would like the meat rare/medium/ well done.	**Ich hätte das Fleisch gerne englisch/medium/ gut durchgebraten.** *ish hètte das flysh gerne english/maydioom/ goot doorsh-gebraten*
Could you heat it up for me, please?	**Könnten Sie mir das bitte nochmal warm machen?** *kernten see meer das bitte nokhmal varm makhen*
I didn't order this.	**Das habe ich nicht bestellt.** *das haabe ish nisht bestellt*
Could you pass me the salt/the oil, please?	**Würden Sie mir bitte das Salz/das Öl geben?** *voorden see meer bitte das salts/das erl gayben*
Do you have any ice creams?	**Haben Sie Eiscreme?** *haaben see ice-kraym*
I would like a sweet/dry sparkling wine.	**Ich hätte gerne einen süßen/trockenen Sekt.** *ish hètte gèrne ighnen soossen/trokkenen sekt*
A liqueur, please.	**Bitte einen Magenbitter.** *bitte ighnen maagen-bitter*
I think there's a mistake on the bill.	**Ich glaube, in der Rechnung ist ein Fehler.** *ish glowbe, in der reshnoongh ist ine fayler*

Could we see the wine list?	**Können wir die Weinkarte haben?** _kernen veer dee vighn-karte haaben_
What wine would you recommend with this dish?	**Welchen Wein empfehlen Sie uns zu diesem Gericht?** _velshen vighn empfaylen see oons tsu deesem gerisht_
Bring us the house wine, please.	**Bringen Sie uns bitte den Hauswein.** _bringen see oons bitte den hows-vighn_
A/half bottle of ...	**Eine/eine halbe Flasche ...** _ighne/ighne halbe flashe ..._
A bottle of still/ sparkling mineral water, please.	**Eine Flasche Mineralwasser ohne/mit Kohlensäure bitte.** _ighne flashe mineraal-vasser one/mit kolen-soyre bitte_
We'd like some unchilled/chilled water.	**Wir hätten gerne nicht zu kaltes/eiskaltes Wasser.** _veer hètten gerne nisht tsoo kaltes/ighskaltes vasser_
Please bring us another bottle of water/wine.	**Bringen Sie uns bitte noch eine Flasche Mineralwasser/Wein.** _bringhen see oons bitte nokh ighne flashe mineraal-vasser/vighn_
Which are the typical local wines/ liquers?	**Welche sind die typischen Weine/Liköre dieser Gegend?** _velshe sint dee toopishen vighne/likerre deeser gaygent_
What liquers do you have?	**Welche Magenbitter/Liköre haben Sie?** _velshe maaghen-bitter/likerre haaben see_

Is there a good restaurant near here?

Gibt es ein gutes Restaurant in dieser Gegend?
gipt es ine gootes restorong in deeser gaygent

Is there a cheap restaurant around here?

Gibt es ein preiswertes Restaurant hier in der Nähe?
gipt es ine prighsvayrtes restorong heer in der nayhe

Can you recommend a restaurant that serves local cuisine?

Können Sie mir ein Restaurant mit regionalen Spezialitäten empfehlen?
kernnen see meer ine restorong mit regionalen shpetsialitèten empfaylen

How can I get there?

Wie kommt man dort hin?
vee komt man dort hin

Excuse me, can you tell me where the ... restaurant is?

Entschuldigung, können Sie mir sagen, wo das Restaurant ... ist?
ent-shooldeegoong, kernnen see meer saagen, vo das restorong ... ist

Which is the best restaurant in town?

Welches ist das beste Restaurant der Stadt?
velshes ist das beste restorong der shtatt

We'd like to have lunch in a cheap restaurant.

Wir würden gern in einem preiswerten Restaurant zu Mittag essen.
veer woorden gern in ighnem prighsverten restorong tsoo mittak essen

EATING OUT - Reservations

Can I book a table for four, please?	**Ist es möglich, einen Tisch für vier Personen zu reservieren?** *ist es merglish, ighnen tish foor feer personen tsoo reserveeren*
I would like to a table for two, for this evening/ tomorrow evening at 8 in the name of...	**Ich möchte einen Tisch für zwei Personen reservieren, für heute/morgen abend um acht auf den Namen ...** *ish mershte ighnen tish foor tsvigh personen reserveeren, foor hoyte/morgen aabent oom akht owf den naamen ...*
What day is it closed?	**An welchem Tag ist Ruhetag?** *an velshem taak ist roohetak*
What time does the restaurant open/ close?	**Wann öffnet/schließt das Restaurant?** *van erffnet/shleest das restorong*
I would like to cancel a booking I made for this evening for two people in the name of ...	**Ich möchte eine Reservierung für heute abend absagen, für zwei Personen auf den Namen ...** *ish mershte ighne reserveeroong foor hoyte aabent ap-saagen, foor tsvigh personen owf den naamen...*
Is it necessary to make a reservation?	**Muß man vorbestellen?** *muss man vor-bestellen*

Excuse me, where is the restroom?

Entschuldigung, wo ist die Toilette?
entshooldeegoong, vo ist dee tolètte

Is there a telephone here?

Gibt es hier ein Telefon?
gipt es heer ine taylayfon

Could I have an ashtray?

Kann ich einen Aschenbecher haben?
kan ish ighnen ashen-bèsher haaben

Could you bring me another glass/plate?

Können Sie mir noch ein Glas/einen Teller bringen?
kernen see meer nokh ine glaas/ighnen teller bringen

Can you change my fork/knife/spoon, please?

Können Sie mir bitte eine neue Gabel/ein neues Messer/einen neuen Löffel geben?
kernen see meer bitte ighne noyer gaabel/ine noyes mèsser/ighnen noyen lerffel geben

Can you turn the heating down/up?

Könnten Sie die Heizung niedriger/höher stellen?
kernten see dee hightsoong needriger/herher shtellen

Is it possible to open/close the window?

Kann man das Fenster öffnen / schließen?
kan man das fenster erffnen/shleessen

I've stained my clothes, do you have a stain-remover?

Ich habe mich bekleckert, haben Sie einen Fleckenentferner?
ish haabe mish beklèkkert, haaben see ighnen flèk-entferner

What time do you close?

Wann schließen Sie?
van sheessen see

Could you call us a taxi, please?

Können Sie uns bitte ein Taxi rufen?
kernen see oons bitte ine taksi rufen

EMERGENCIES

Is there a doctor here?

Gibt es hier einen Arzt?
gipt es heer ighnen arzt

Call a doctor/an
ambulance!

**Rufen Sie einen Arzt/einen
Krankenwagen!**
*roofen see ighnen arzt/ighnen
kranken-vaagen*

Go and get help,
quickly!

Rufen Sie Hilfe, schnell!
roofen see hilfe, shnèll

My wife is about
to give birth.

Meine Frau liegt in den Wehen.
mine frow leegt in den vayhen

Where is the nearest
police station/
hospital?

**Wo ist die nächste Polizeistation/das
nächste Krankenhaus?**
*vo ist dee nèxte politsigh-shtatsioon/
das nèxte kranken-hows*

I've lost my credit
card/wallet.

**Ich habe meine Kreditkarte/meine
Brieftasche verloren.**
*ich haabe mine kredeet-karte/mine
breef-tashe ferloren*

I've been robbed.

Ich bin beraubt worden.
ich bin berowpt vorden

My wallet has been
stolen.

**Meine Brieftasche ist gestohlen
worden.**
mine breef-tashe ist geshtolen vorden

I've lost my son/my
daughter.

**Ich habe meinen Sohn/meine
Tochter verloren.**
*ich haabe mighnen sont/mine
tokhter ferloren*

Are they any nightclubs?	**Gibt es Nachtlokale?** *gipt es nakht-lok<u>aa</u>le*
Is there somewhere/ a show suitable for children?	**Gibt es einen Ort/eine Veranstaltung für Kinder?** *gipt es <u>igh</u>nen ort/<u>i</u>ne fer<u>a</u>nshtaltoong foor k<u>i</u>nder*
What is there to do in the evenings?	**Was kann man abends machen?** *vas kan man <u>aa</u>benz m<u>à</u>khen*
Where is there a cinema/a theater?	**Wo ist ein Kino/ein Theater?** *voo ist <u>i</u>ne keeno/<u>i</u>ne tay<u>ah</u>ter*
Can you book the tickets for us?	**Können Sie uns die Eintrittskarten reservieren?** *kernen see oons dee <u>igh</u>ntriz-k<u>a</u>rten reserv<u>ee</u>ren*
Is there a swimming pool?	**Gibt es ein Schwimmbad?** *gipt es <u>i</u>ne shvim-baat*
Are there any good excursions to take?	**Kann man schöne Ausflüge machen?** *kan man sherne <u>ows</u>flooge m<u>a</u>khen*
Where can we play tennis/golf?	**Wo können wir Tennis/Golf spielen?** *vo kernnen veer t<u>è</u>nnis/golf shp<u>ee</u>len*
Is there horseriding/ fishing?	**Kann man hier reiten/angeln gehen?** *kan man heer r<u>igh</u>ten/<u>a</u>ngeln gayhen*

FOOD SHOPPING

Things to remember

For the most interesting shopping expeditions, the signs you are looking for are: Konditorei (cakeshop), Bäckerei (baker's), Metzgerei (butcher's), Weinhandlung (wine merchant's) and Feinkostgeschäfte (delicatessen). The larger supermarkets also sell some excellent produce.

How much does it cost per kilo?	**Wieviel kostet das pro Kilo?** *veefeel kostet das pro keelo*
How long will it keep?	**Wie lange ist das haltbar?** *vee langeh ist das haltbaar*
I'll take this.	**Ich nehme dies.** *ish nayme dees*
I'd like two bottles (of it).	**Ich hätte gern zwei Flaschen davon.** *ish hètte gern tsvigh flashen dafon*
Give me half a kilo of it.	**Geben Sie mir ein halbes Kilo davon** *gayben see meer ine halbes keelo dafon*
Can you wrap it up for the journey?	**Können Sie mir das für die Reise verpacken?** *kernen see meer das foor dee rayse ferpaken*

THE DEFINITE ARTICLE

In German there are three genders: masculine, feminine and neuter; singular and plural; four declensions: nominative, genitive, dative, accusative. In the plural, the declension of the definite article is the same for all three genders.

	Singular		Plural
	Masculine	Feminine	Neuter
Nominative	der Mann	die Frau	das Kind	die Kinder
Genitive	des Mannes	der Frau	des Kindes	der Kinder
Dative	dem Mann	der Frau	dem Kind	den Kindern
Accusative	den Mann	die Frau	das Kind	die Kinder

THE INDEFINITE ARTICLE

The indefinite article follows the definite. They are the same for the masculine and the neuter.

	Masculine	Feminine	Neuter
Nominative	ein Mann	eine Frau	ein Kind
Genitive	eines Mannes	einer Frau	eines Kindes
Dative	einem Mann	einer Frau	einem Kind
Accusative	einen Mann	eine Frau	ein Kind

Personal pronouns follow the same pattern: **mein** (my), **dein** (your), **sein** (his/her), **unser** (our), **euer** (your), **ihr** (their) and **kein** (no-one).

NOUNS

German nouns are always capitalized. Most of them decline as shown in the table for the definite article above (note the **s** (or **es**) of the singular genitive for masculine and neuter nouns and the **n** in the plural dative for all nouns). There are no hard and fast rules determining gender, but remember: nouns ending in **-ung**, **-keit**,

-heit, **-schaft** are feminine; verb nouns are neuter; diminutives
(i.e. **-chen** and **-lein**) are all neuter.

There is no fixed rule for the plural either; plural nouns may take
-n -e -en -er -ern, etc. (and/or the dieresis).

E.g.:

der Preis	die Prei**se**
die Stadt	die St**ä**dt**e**
das Haus	die H**äu**s**er**

ADJECTIVES

Predicative adjectives remain unchanged regardless of gender
and quantity.

E.g.:

The bicycle is **new**.	Das Fahrrad ist **neu**.
The bicycles are **new**.	Die Fahrräder sind **neu**.

Qualifying adjectives always come before the noun; the form
varies according to the gender, number and declension of the
noun. When preceded by the definite article it takes the ending **-n**
o **-en** or **-e** (in the nominative singular, the feminine accusative
and the neuter singular).

E.g.:

The old man	Der alt**e** Mann
The old men	Die alt**en** Männer

Demonstrative adjectives follow the declension of the definite
article.

this = dies**er**, dies**e**, dies**es**
that = jen**er**, jen**e**, jen**es**
these = dies**e**
those = jen**e**

PRONOUNS

Personal pronouns:

Nominative		Dative		Accusative	
I	= **ich**	to me	= **mir**	me	= **mich**
you	= **du**	to you	= **dir**	you	= **dich**
he	= **er**	to him	= **ihm**	him	= **ihn**
she	= **sie**	to her	= **ihr**	her	= **sie**
it	= **es**	to it	= **ihm**	it	= **es**
we	= **wir**	to us	= **uns**	us	= **uns**
you	= **ihr**	to you	= **euch**	you	= **euch**
they	= **sie**	to them	= **ihnen**	them	= **sie**
you	= **Sie**	to you	= **Ihnen**	you	= **Sie**
(formal)					

Interrogatives:

	Nominative	Accusative
who?	**wer?**	**wen**
which?	**welcher,-e,-es**	**welchen,-e,-es**
what?	**was?**	**was?**

PREPOSITIONS

Prepositions which take the genitive:
statt (instead of), **während** (during), **trotz** (notwithstanding),
wegen (because of);
Prepositions which take the dative:
aus (outside), **bei** (near), **gegenüber** (opposite), **mit** (with), **nach**
(after), **seit** (from), **von** (from, of), **zu** (to);
Prepositions which take the accusative:
bis (until), **durch** (across), **für** (for), **gegen** (against), **ohne**
(without), **um** (around);
Prepositions which take the dative if the verb is stationary, and
the accusative if the verb is of motion:
an (near), **auf** (on), **hinter** (behind), **in** (in), **neben** (near), **über**
(above), **unter** (under, among), **vor** (in front of), **zwischen** (between).

VERBS

There are two groups of verbs in German:
weak or regular: conjugation is regular in all tenses and modes;
strong or irregular: irregular in the simple past, past participle,
present indicative and imperative.

REGULAR CONJUGATION:

Present (to say - sagen)

I say	**ich sage**
you say	**du sagst**
he/she/it says	**er/sie/es sagt**
we say	**wir sagen**
you say	**ihr sagt**
they say	**sie sagen**

Present perfect (composed of an auxiliary verb - haben [to have],
sein [to be] - and the past participle, which goes at the end of the
sentence.)

I have said	**ich habe ... gesagt**
you have said	**du hast ... gesagt**
he/she/it said	**er/sie/es hat ... gesagt**
we have said	**wir haben ... gesagt**
you have said	**ihr habt ... gesagt**
they have said	**sie haben ... gesagt**

Simple past (the ending of the infinitive is replaced by a **t** and the
verb is conjugated as follows:)

I said/was saying	**ich sagte**
you said	**du sagtest**
he said	**er/sie/es sagte**
we said	**wir sagten**
you said	**ihr sagtet**
they said	**sie sagten**

Irregular verbs change the vowel in the simple past and in the past particilpe.

E.g.:

Infinitive	Simple past 1st sing.	Past participle
bitten (to pray)	ich bat	gebeten
essen (to eat)	ich aß	gegessen
geben (to give)	ich gab	gegeben
kommen (to come)	ich kam	gekommen
schlafen (to sleep)	ich schlief	geschlafen
trinken (to drink)	ich trank	getrunken

Auxiliary verbs: there are three auxiliary verbs in German, **haben** (to have) and **sein** (to be) are used (together with the past participle which goes at the end of the sentence) to form the present perfect, and **werden** (to become) which is used (together with the infinitive which goes at the end of the sentence) to form the future (**ich werde gehen** = I will go) and (with the past participle) the passive (**das Kind wird umarmt** = the baby is hugged).

sein (to be)	**haben** (to have)	**werden** (to become)
ich bin	**ich habe**	**ich werde**
du bist	**du hast**	**du wirst**
er ist	**er hat**	**er wird**
wir sind	**wir haben**	**wir werden**
ihr seid	**ihr habt**	**ihr werdet**
sie sind	**sie haben**	**sie werden**

Simple past of the auxiliary verbs:
ich war (I was), **ich hatte** (I had), **ich wurde** (I became).

N.B.: the polite 'you' form in German is expressed with the third person **'Sie'** and is the same in the singular and the plural.

GREETINGS

Hi	**Hallo, Servus** *hallo, sèrvus*
Hello	**Guten Tag** *gooten taak*
Good morning	**Guten Morgen** *gooten morgen*
Good evening	**Guten Abend** *gooten aabent*
Good night	**Gute Nacht** *goote nakht*
Goodbye/See you soon/Bye!	**Auf Wiedersehen/Bis bald! Tschüs!** *auf veeder-sayhen/bis balt! choos*
Pleased to meet you!	**Angenehm!** *anghenaym*
How are you?	**Wie geht's?** *vee ghayts*
Fine, thanks.	**Gut, danke.** *goot, danke*
Please	**Bitte** *bitte*
Excuse me/I'm sorry	**Entschuldigung/Es tut mir leid** *ent-shooldeegoong/es toot meer light*
Thank you very much	**Vielen Dank** *feelen dank*
Yes please/No thank you	**Ja, bitte/Nein, danke** *yaa, bitte/nine, danke*
I/We would like	**Ich möchte/wir möchten...** *ish mershte/veer mershten ...*

I'd like to book a single/double room.

Ich möchte ein Einzel-/Doppelzimmer reservieren.
ish mershte ine ighntsel-/doppel-tsimmer reserveeren

I'd like a room with breakfast/half board/full board.

Ich möchte ein Zimmer mit Frühstück/Halbpension/Vollpension.
ish mershte ine tsimmer mit frooshtook/halp-pangsion/ foll-pangsion

How much is it per night/week?

Wieviel kostet es pro Tag/pro Woche?
veefeel kostet es pro taak/pro vokhe

Does the price include breakfast?

Ist das Frühstück im Preis inbegriffen?
ist das frooshtook im prise inbe-griffen

We will be staying for three nights from... to...

Wir bleiben drei Nächte vom ... bis zum ...
veer blighben drigh nèshte fom ... bis zoom ...

We will arrive at ... o'clock

Wir kommen um ... an.
veer kommen oom ... an

We have booked a room in the name of...

Wir haben ein Zimmer auf den Namen ... reserviert.
veer haben ine tsimmer owf den namen ... reserveert

Can you have my bags brought up to my room?

Können Sie mein Gepäck bitte auf's Zimmer bringen lassen?
kernnen see mine gepèk bitte owfs tsimmer bringhen lassen

What time is breakfast/lunch/dinner?	**Um wieviel Uhr gibt es Frühstück/Mittagessen/Abendessen?** *oom veefeel oor gipt es frooshtook/mittak-essen /abent-essen*
We would like breakfast/a bottle of wine in our room.	**Wir hätten gern das Frühstück/eine Flasche Wein auf unserem Zimmer.** *veer hètten gern das frooshtook/ighne flashe vine owf oonserem tsimmer*
Can I have my key?	**Kann ich meinen Schlüssel haben?** *kan ish mighnen shloossel haaben*
Please put it on my bill.	**Schreiben Sie es bitte auf meine Rechnung.** *shrighben see es bitte owf mine reshnoong*
Can I have another blanket/pillow?	**Kann ich noch eine Decke/ein Kopfkissen bekommen?** *kan ish nokh ighne dèkke/ine kopf-kìssen bekommen*
I'm locked out of my room.	**Ich habe mich aus meinem Zimmer ausgesperrt.** *ish habe mish ows mighnem tsimmer ows-geshpèrrt*

NUMBERS

0	null	*nool*	
1	eins	*ines*	
2	zwei	*tsvigh*	
3	drei	*drigh*	
4	vier	*feer*	
5	fünf	*foonf*	
6	sechs	*sekhs*	
7	sieben	*seeben*	
8	acht	*akht*	
9	neun	*noyn*	
10	zehn	*tsayn*	
11	elf	*elf*	
12	zwölf	*tsverlf*	
13	dreizehn	*drigh-tsayn*	
14	vierzehn	*feer-tsayn*	
15	fünfzehn	*foonf-tsayn*	
16	sechzehn	*saysh-tsayn*	
17	siebzehn	*seep-tsayn*	
18	achtzehn	*akht-tsayn*	
19	neunzehn	*noyn-tsayn*	
20	zwanzig	*tsvantsik*	
21	einundzwanzig	*ine-oont-tsvantsik*	
22	zweiundzwanzig	*tsvigh-oont-tsvantsik*	
23	dreiundzwanzig	*drigh-oont-tsvantsik*	
30	dreißig	*drighssik*	
40	vierzig	*feertsik*	
50	fünfzig	*foonftsik*	

60	sechzig	*sayshtsik*
70	siebzig	*seeptsik*
80	achzig	*akhtsik*
90	neunzig	*noyntsik*
100	hundert	*hoondert*
101	hundertundeins	*hoondert-oont-ighntz*
102	hundertzwei	*hoondert-tsvigh*
110	hundertzehn	*hoondert-tsayn*
200	zweihundert	*tsvigh-hoondert*
300	dreihundert	*drigh-hoondert*
1000	tausend	*towsent*
2000	zweitausend	*tsvigh-towsent*
1000000	eine Million	*ighne mileeon*

1 st	erster	*èrster*
2 nd	zweiter	*tsvighter*
3 rd	dritter	*dritter*
4 th	vierter	*feerter*
5 th	fünfter	*foonfter*
6 th	sechster	*sekhster*
7 th	siebter	*seepter*
8 th	achter	*akhter*
9 th	neunter	*noynter*
10 th	zehnter	*tsaynter*

123

PAYING THE BILL

Things to remember

Major credit cards are accepted in most shops, hotels and restaurants in large cities and popular tourist destinations, but not as widespread as in the U.K. or the States. Check the signs at the door to see which credit cards are accepted.

How much is it?	**Wieviel kostet das?** *veefeel kostet das*
Can I have the bill, please?	**Bringen Sie mir bitte die Rechnung.** *bringen see meer bitte dee reshnung*
Can I pay by credit card?	**Kann ich mit Kreditkarte bezahlen?** *kan ish mit kredeet-karte betsaalen*
Do you accept checks/ traveler's cheques?	**Nehmen Sie Schecks/Reiseschecks?** *naymen see shèks/righse-shèks*
Can I have the receipt, please?	**Geben Sie mir bitte eine Quittung.** *geben see meer bitte ighne kvitoong*
Is VAT included?	**Ist die Mehrwertsteuer inbegriffen?** *ist dee mayrvert-shtoyer ighnbegriffen*
What is the total?	**Was macht das zusammen?** *vas makht das tsoosammen*
Do I have to leave a deposit?	**Muß ich eine Anzahlung leisten?** *mooss ish ighne an-tsaaloong lighsten*
I think you have given me the wrong change.	**Ich glaube, Sie haben mir falsch herausgegeben.** *ish glowbe, see haben meer falsh herows-gegayben.*

Can you help me, please?
Können Sie mir bitte helfen?
kernnen see meer bitte helfen

What's the matter?
Was ist los?
vas ist loos

What has happened?
Was ist passiert?
vas ist passeert

I need help.
Ich brauche Hilfe.
ish browkhe hilfe

I don't understand.
Ich verstehe Sie nicht.
ish fershtayhe see nisht

I'd like an interpreter.
Ich hätte gerne einen Dolmetscher.
ish hètte gerne ighnen dolmèsher

Say it again, please.
Können Sie das bitte wiederholen?
kernen see das bitte veeder-holen

I've got no money left.
Ich habe kein Geld mehr.
ish haabe kighn gelt mayr

I can't find my son/my daughter.
Ich kann meinen Sohn/meine Tochter nicht mehr finden.
ish kan mighnen son/mighne tokhter nisht mayr finden

I'm lost.
Ich habe mich verlaufen.
ish haabe mish ferlowfen

Leave me alone!
Laß mich in Ruhe!
lass mish in roohe

PRONUNCIATION

German pronunciation should not pose too many problems for the native English-speaker. There may only be a few surprising sounds if this your first visit to a German-speaking country. To help you use this guide and give you the courage to conduct your first converstions in German, you will find a guide to pronunciation in italics after each word or phrase. Reading these 'Anglicized' phonetics as if they were English, you should be able to produce convincing German pronunciation and have no trouble making yourself understood. After a little practice these sound will be tripping naturally off your tongue.

Double vowels are sounded long, while a double consonant shortens the preceding vowel. Particularly long words have been hyphenated to aid reading, but should be read together. The underlined syllable indicates where the stress falls.

German spelling	English pronunciation	Phonetic spelling
ä	e, as in bed	è
au	ow as in how	ow
äu, eu	oy, as in boy	oy
ei	igh, as in high	igh/i
ie	ee	ee
ö	er as in pert	er
ü	oo as in food	oo
ch	ch as in the Scottish loch. When preceded by a, o, u it is quite hard, softer when preceded by e, i, ö, ü	kh / sh
sch	sh as in show	sh
st, sp	before t and p, s is pronounced sh	sht, shp
tsch	ch is in chill	ch
ß	double ss	ss
w	v as in vase	v
v	f as in four	f
g	always hard as in got, never as in gem	g

Things to remember

Some religious holidays are regional, or limited to towns
where the majority of the population is Catholic.

New Year's Eve	**Silvester** *silvèster*
New Year's Day	**Neujahr** *noy-yar*
Epiphany (6 January)	**Dreikönigsfest** *drigh-kerniks-fest*
Good Friday	**Karfreitag** *karfrightak*
Easter	**Ostern** *ostern*
Easter Monday	**Ostermontag** *oster-montak*
1st May	**Tag der Arbeit** *taak der arbight*
Ascension	**Christi Himmelfahrt** *kristi himmel-faart*
Pentecost	**Pfingsten** *pfingsten*
Corpus Domini	**Fronleichnam** *fron-lighshnam*

Assumption of the
Virgin

Mariä Himmelfahrt
maree-è himmelfaart

Unification of
Germany (3 October)

Tag der deutschen Einheit
taak der doytshen ighnhight

All Saints' Day
(1 November)

Allerheiligen
aller-highleegen

Day of penitence
and prayer
(the first Wednesday after All
Souls' Day, 2 November)

Buß- und Bettag
booss oont bayt-taak

Christmas Eve

Heiligabend
highleek-abent

Christmas

1. Weihnachtstag
erster vigh-nakhts-taak

Boxing Day

2. Weihnachtstag
tsvighter vighnakhts-taak

Is it far? | **Ist es weit?**
ist es vight

Is it expensive? | **Ist es teuer?**
ist es toyer

Have you understood? | **Haben Sie verstanden?**
haaben see fershtanden

Can you help me? | **Können Sie mir helfen?**
kernnen see meer hèlfen

Where are the shops? | **Wo sind die Geschäfte?**
vo sint dee geshèfte

How do I get there? | **Wie kommt man dahin?**
vee komt man dahin

What is this? | **Was ist das?**
vas ist das

Where? | **Wo?**
vo

When? | **Wann?**
van

What? | **Was?**
vas

Why? | **Warum?**
varoom

RESTROOMS

Things to remember

> In Germany especially you may find public toilets (for example on the motorway) which are coin operated. Sometimes there will be a cleaning lady who will glare at you if you fail to add a coin to the saucer of money in front of her. So therefore it is a good idea to keep a few coins in your pocket at all times.

Where is the restroom, please?
Wo ist die Toilette, bitte?
vo ist dee tolètte, bitte

Do you have to pay for the toilets?
Kostet die Toilette etwas?
kostet dee tolètte etvas

There is no toilet paper/soap.
Es gibt kein Toilettenpapier/keine Seife.
es gipt kighn tolètten-papeer/kighne sighfe

Is there a toilet for the disabled?
Gibt es eine Behindertentoilette?
gipt es ighne behinderten-tolètte

The toilet is blocked.
Das W.C. ist verstopft.
das vay-zay ist fershtopft

Things to remember

In Austria, Germany and Switzerland there is no smoking in public places (cinemas, theaters, public transport); there are smoking compartments on some trains. Smoking is generally allowed in restaurants and pubs, unless it specifically forbidden. Some restaurants have no smoking areas. If there is no ashtray on your table, you are probably in a no smoking area.

s smoking allowed here?	**Darf man hier rauchen?** *darf man heer rowkhen*
Do you mind if I smoke?	**Stört es Sie, wenn ich rauche?** *sterrt es see, ven ish rowkhe*
Could I have an ashtray?	**Kann ich einen Aschenbecher haben?** *kan ish ighnen ashen-bèsher haaben*
Do you have any matches?	**Haben Sie Streichhölzer?** *haaben see shtrighsh-herlzer*
Have you got a light?	**Haben Sie Feuer?** *haaben see foyer*
Would you mind not smoking?	**Würde es Ihnen etwas ausmachen, nicht zu rauchen?** *woorde es eenen ètvas owsmakhen, nisht tsoo rowkhen*

TAXIS

Can you call me a taxi please?	**Können Sie bitte ein Taxi rufen?** _kernen see bitte ine taksi rufen_
To the main station/ airport.	**Zum Bahnhof/zum Flughafen.** _tsoom baanhof/zoom flook-haafen_
Take me to this address/this hotel.	**Bringen Sie mich zu dieser Adresse/zu diesem Hotel.** _bringen see mish tsoo deeser adresse/tsoo deesem hotel_
Is it far?	**Ist es weit?** _ist es vight_
I'm in a hurry.	**Ich habe es sehr eilig.** _ish haabe es sayr ighlik_
How much will it cost?	**Wieviel wird es kosten?** _vifeel veert es kosten_
Stop here/at the corner.	**Halten Sie hier/an der Ecke.** _halten see heer/an der ekke_
How much is it?	**Was kostet das?** _vas kostet das_
Could you give me a receipt?	**Können Sie mir eine Quittung schreiben?** _kernen see meer ine kvittoong shrighben_
Keep the change.	**Behalten Sie den Rest.** _behalten see den rest_

Things to remember

In all three countries you can call from public telephones using coins or phonecards. In Austria the telephones take 1, 5 or 10 schilling coins which are not worth much for international calls, so make sure you have a large supply of change. Phonecards are becoming more commonplace and come in denominations of 50 and 100 schillings. In Germany coin-operated telephones are becoming increasingly rare, but those left take 10 or 50 Pfenning and 1 or 5 mark coins (one unit costs 30 Pfennings). Phonecards cost 12 or 50 marks and can be bought at post offices and telephone shops. In Switzerland, the telephones take all coins, except the tiny 5 centimes coin, but even a local call will cost at least 50 centimes. Phonecards can be bought for 2, 5 and 10 Swiss francs, and some companies give them away as prizes.

Is there a phone?	**Gibt es ein Telefon?** *gipt es ine taylayfon*
I'd like an outside line.	**Geben Sie mir eine Freileitung?** *gayben see meer ighne frigh-lightoong*
Give me a 12-mark phonecard, please.	**Geben Sie mir bitte eine Telefonkarte zu 12 Mark.** *gayben see meer bitte ighne taylayfon-karte tsoo tsverlf mark*
I'd like to make a telephone call.	**Ich möchte gerne telefonieren.** *ish mershte gerne taylayfoneeren*
The number is ..., extension ...	**Die Nummer ist ..., Durchwahl ...** *dee noomer ist ..., doorsh-vaal ...*

| I can't get through. | **Ich komme nicht durch.** |
| | *ish komme nisht doorsh* |

| What is the prefix for ...? | **Wie lautet die Vorwahl von ...** |
| | *vee lowtet dee forvaal fon ...* |

| Can you give me change in 5/10 schilling coins? | **Können Sie mir das in Münzen zu 5/10 Schilling wechseln?** |
| | *kernen see meer das in moonzen zoo foonf/tsayn shilling vexeln* |

| It's busy. | **Die Leitung ist besetzt.** |
| | *dee lightoong ist besezt* |

| Hello, this is ... | **Hallo, hier spricht ...** |
| | *hallo, heer shprisht ...* |

| Can I speak to ...? | **Kann ich mit ... sprechen?** |
| | *kan ish mit ... shpreshen* |

| I've been cut off. | **Die Verbindung ist unterbrochen worden.** |
| | *dee fèrbindoong ist oonterbrokhen vorden* |

| Sorry, wrong number. | **Entschuldigung, ich habe mich verwählt.** |
| | *ent-shooldeegoong, ish haabe mish fervèlt* |

| It's a bad line. | **Ich kann Sie schlecht verstehen.** |
| | *ish kan see shlèsht fershtayhen* |

YOU MAY HEAR:

Hallo, wer spricht da?
hallo, ver shprisht da

Hello, who's speaking?

Bleiben Sie am Apparat.
blighben see am aparat

Hold the line.

**Probieren Sie es bitte
später noch einmal.**
*probeeren see es bitte
shpèter nokh ighnmal*

Please call back later.

**Er/sie ist nicht zu
Hause/nicht da.**
*er/see ist nisht tsoo
howse/nisht da*

He/She is not at home/not here.

Sie haben sich verwählt.
see haaben sish ferwèlt

You've got the wrong number.

TIME 1

What time is it?	**Wieviel Uhr ist es?** *veefeel oor ist es*
It's ...	**Es ist ...** *es ist ...*
8.00	**acht Uhr** *akht oor*
8.05	**fünf nach acht** *foonf nach akht*
8.10	**zehn nach acht** *tsayn nach akht*
8.15	**Viertel nach acht** *feertel nach akht*
8.20	**zwanzig nach acht** *tsvantsik nach akht*
8.30	**halb neun** *halp noyn*
8.40	**zwanzig vor neun** *tsvantsik for noyn*
8.45	**Viertel vor neun** *feertel for noyn*
8.50	**zehn vor neun** *tsayn for noyn*
Eight AM/PM	**acht Uhr morgens/abends** *akht oor morghents/aabents*

Midday	**zwölf Uhr mittags** *zverlf oor mìttakhs*
Midnight	**zwölf Uhr nachts** *zverlf oor nakhts*
What time do you open/close?	**Um wieviel Uhr öffnen/schließen Sie?** *oom veefeel oor erffnen/shleessen see*
What time does the restaurant close?	**Um wieviel Uhr schließt das Restaurant?** *oom veefeel oor shleest das restorong*
What time do the shops close?	**Um wieviel Uhr schließen die Geschäfte?** *oom veefeel oor shleessen de geshèfte*
How long will it take to get there?	**Wie lange fährt man dahin?** *vee lange fayrt man dahin*
We arrived early/late.	**Wir sind zu früh/zu spät.** *veer sint tsu froo/tsu shpayt*
It is early/late.	**Es ist früh/spät.** *es ist froo/shpayt*
What time does the bus leave?	**Um wieviel Uhr fährt der Bus ab?** *oom veefeel oor fayrt der boos ap*
The table is booked for ... (o'clock) this evening.	**Der Tisch ist für ... Uhr heute abend reserviert.** *der teesh ist foor ... oor hoyte abent reserveert*

WEIGHTS AND MEASURES

Half a liter of ...

Einen halben Liter ...
ighnen halben leeter ...

A kilo of ...

Ein Kilo ...
ine keelo ...

Half a kilo of ...

Ein halbes Kilo ...
ine halbes keelo ...

100 grams of ...

100 g ...
hoondert gram ...

A slice of ... (cake)

Eine Scheibe ... /Ein Stück (Kuchen)
ighne shighbe .../ine shtook (kukhen)

A portion of ...

Eine Portion ...
ighne portsion ...

A dozen ...

Ein Dutzend ...
ine dutsent

Two marks' worth of ...

Zu zwei Mark ...
zu zvai mark ...

DICTIONARY OF GASTRONOMIC TERMS

We have included the corresponding articles with the German nouns to show their gender (e.g. der=masculine; die=feminine; das=neuter).

above auf *owf*, über *oober*

additive zusätzlich *tsoosètslish*

address die Adresse *adrèsse*

adult erwachsen *ervaksen*, der Erwachsene *erwaksene*

aeroplane das Flugzeug *fluktsoyk*

after nach(her) *naakh(her)*

after-dinner liqueur verdauungsfördernd *ferdowoongs-ferrdernt*, Magenbitter *maagen-bìtter*

against gegen *gegen*

air die Luft *looft*; **air conditioning** die Klimaanlage *kleemaanlage*

airport der Flughafen *flukhaafen*

à la carte nach der Karte *nakh der karte*

alcoholic alkoholhaltig *alkohol-haltig*

alcoholic drinks alkoholische Getränke *alkoholishe getrènk*

all alles *alles*

allergy die Allergie *allèrgee*

almonds die Mandeln *mandeln*

also auch *owkh*

always immer *immer*

anchovy die Sardelle *sardèlle*

aniseed der Anis *anees*

antibiotic das Antibiotikum *antibeeoti-koom*

anyone irgend jemand *eergent yemant*

aperitif der Aperitif *aperiteef*

appetite der Appetit *appeteet*

appetizer die Vorspeise *forshpighse*

apple der Apfel *apfel*

appointment die Verabredung *fèrabredoong*

apricot die Aprikose *aprikose*

April der April *april*

aroma das Aroma *aroma*,
der Geschmack *geshmak*

aromatic aromatisch
aromatish, geschmackvoll
gheshmakfoll

around umher *oomher*,
ringsumher *rings-oomher*

arrive, to ankommen
ankommen

artichoke die Artischocke
artishokke

ash die Asche *ashe*

ashtray der Aschenbecher
ashen-bèsher

ask, to fragen *fragen*

asparagus der Spargel
spargel

aspirin das Aspirin *aspirin*

at least wenigstens
venikstens

au gratin überbacken
ooberbakken

August der August *owgoost*

Austria Österreich *erster-
righsh*

Austrian österreichisch
erster-righshish, der
Österreicher *erster-
righsher*

authentic echt *èsht*, wahr
var

avocado die Avokado
avokado

avoid, to vermeiden
fermighden

baby das Kind *kint*

backwards rückwärts
rookvèrz, zurück *zoorook*

bacon der Speck *shpèk*;
smoked bacon
geräucherter
Schinkenspeck
*geroysherter shinken-
shpèk*

bad böse *berse*, schlecht
shlèsht, schlimm *shlim*,
das Übel *oobel*

bag die Tasche *tashe*

banana die Banane *banane*

bank die Bank *bank*

bar das Lokal *lokaal*, das
Café *cafay*

barley die Gerste *gèrste*;
pearl barley die Graupen
growpen

barman der Barmixer
barmìxer

basil das Basilikum
basilikoom

Basle Basel *baasel*

batter der Teig *tighk*

Bavarian bayerisch _bayrish_

Baveria Bayern _bayern_

bay leaf der Lorbeer _lorber_

beans weiße Bohnen _vighsse bonen_

beautiful schön _shern_

because warum _varoom_, weil _vighl_

beef das Rind _rint_

beer das Bier _beer_

beetroot die Rote Bete _rote bayte_

before zuerst _tsooerst_

begin, to anfangen _anfangen_

beginning der Anfang _anfang_

behind hinter _hìnter_, dahinter _dahìnter_

bell pepper die Paprika _paprika_

belly ache die Bauchschmerzen _bowkh-shmèrtsen_

Berlin Berlin _berlin_

berry die Beere _bayre_

better beste(r) _beste(r)_, besser _besser_

between zwischen _tsvìshen_

big groß _gross_, herrlich _hèrlish_

bill die Rechnung _rèshnoong_, das Konto _konto_

biscuits die Kekse _kekse_

bitter bitter _bìtter_, der Magenbitter _màagenbitter_

bitters (liqueur) die Sauerkirsche _sowerkeershe_

black schwarz _shvarts_

blend die Mischung _mishoong_

blood das Blut _bloot_

blueberries die Heidelbeeren _highdelbayeren_

boil, to kochen _kokhen_

boiled gekocht _gekokht_, Koch- _kokh_

boiling kochend _kokhent_

bone die Knochen _knokhen_

book das Buch _bookh_

book, to vorbestellen _forbeshtèllen_, reservieren _reserveeren_

bottle die Flasche _flashe_

bottle-opener der Flaschenöffner _flashen-öffner_

bottled (in Flaschen) abgefüllt _(in flashen) apgefoollt_

box die Schachtel *shakhtel*

boy der Junge *yoonge*

brain das Hirn *heern*

braised geschmort *geshmort*, der Schmorbraten *shmor-braten*

bread das Brot *brot*

breadcrumbs das Paniermehl *paneermayl*

breaded paniert *paneert*

bread roll das Brötchen *brertshen*

break, to zerbrechen *tserbreshen*

breakfast das Frühstück *frooshtook*

breast die Brust *broost*

broad beans dicke (Sau)bohnen *dikke (sow)-bonen*

broccoli der Brokkoli *brokkolee*

broken kaputt *kapoott*

brush die Bürste *boorste*

Brussels sprouts der Rosenkohl *rosen-kol*

buggy der Kinderwagen *kinder-vagen*

burn, to brennen *brènnen* verbrennen *ferbrènnen*

burnt verbrannt *ferbrant*, angebrannt *an-gebrant*

bus der Bus *boos*; **(bus) stop** die Haltestelle *halte-shtèlle*

busy besetzt *besètst*

butcher die Metzgerei *mèz-gerigh*

butter die Butter *booter*

buttered mit Butter bestrichen *mit booter beshtrishen*

button der Knopf *knopf*

buy, to kaufen *kowfen*

by bei *bigh*

cabbage der Kohl *kol*

caffellatte der Milchkaffee *milsh-kaffay*

cake der Kuchen *kookhen*; **layer cake** die Torte *torte*

cakeshop die Konditorei *konditorigh*

call (telephone) der Telefonanruf *telefon-anroof*

call, to (an)rufen *(an)roofen*

calm ruhig *roohig/ roohish*

calming beruhigend *beroohigent*

calories die Kalorien *kaloree-en*

camomile die Kamille *kameelle*, der Kamillentee *kameellen-tay*

can (be able to) können *kernnen*

cancel, to auslöschen *owslershen*, absagen *absagen*

candied fruit kandierte Früchte *kandeerte frooshte*

candle die Kerze *kèrtse*

can-opener der Dosenöffner *dosen-erffner*

capers die Kapern *kapern*

capon der Kapaun *kapawn*

caraffe die Karaffe *karaffe*

caramel der Karamel *karamèl*

carbonated mit Kohlensäure *mìt kolensoyre*

careful vorsichtig *forsishtik*

carpark der Parkplatz *parkplats*

carrot die Möhre *mer-re*, Karotte *karotte*

carry, to tragen *traagen*

cart der Karren *karren*

cash das Bargeld *bargèlt*

cashier die Kassiererin *kasseererin*

cauliflower der Blumenkohl *bloomen-kol*

caviar der Kaviar *kaviar*

celery der Sellerie *sèlleree*

cellar der (Wein)Keller *(vighn)-kèller*

center das Zentrum *tsèntroom*

central zentral *tsentral*

cereals das Getreide *getrighde*

chair der Stuhl *shtool*

chambermaid das Zimmermädchen *tsimmer-mèdshen*

champagne der Champagner *shampanyer*

change das Kleingeld *klighn-ghelt*

change, to wechseln *vèxeln*

chard der Mangold *mangolt*

cheap preiswert, *prighsvert*

check (U.K. cheque) der Scheck *shèk*

cheers! Prost! *prost* Prosit! *prosit* Zum Wohl! *tsoom vol*

cheese der Käse *kèse*

cherry die Kirsche *keershe*

chestnut die (Eß)Kastanie *(ès)-kastani-e*

chestnuts die Eßkastanien *èss-kast_a_neeyen*, Maronen *mar_o_nen*

chew, to kauen *k_o_wen*

chicken das Huhn *hoon*

chickpeas die Kichererbsen *kisher-èrpsen*

chili pepper der Peperoni *peper_o_nee*

chill, to abkühlen *abkoolen*

chips (crisps) die Kartoffelchips *kart_o_ffel-chips*

chocolate die Schokolade *shokol_a_de*; **hot chocolate** heiße Schokolade *highsse shokol_a_de*; **chocolate (praline)** die Praline *pral_i_ne*, das Konfekt *konf_è_kt*

chop das Rippenstück *rippen-shtook,* das Rippchen *ripp-shen*

chop, to kleinhacken *kl_igh_nhakken*

Christmas Weihnachten *v_igh_nakhten*

cigar die Zigarre *tsig_a_rre*

cigarette die Zigarette *tsigar_è_tte*

cinnamon der Zimt *tsìmt*

citrus fruit die Zitrusfrucht *zìtrus-frookht*

citty die Stadt *shtat*

clean sauber *s_o_wber*

clear hell *hèll*, klar *claar*

client der Kunde *k_o_onde*

cloakroom die Garderobe *garder_o_be*

clock die Uhr *oor*

close, to schließen *shl_ee_sser*

closed geschlossen *geshl_o_ssen*, zu *tsoo*

closing time die Schließung *shl_ee_ssoong*

coat der Mantel *m_a_ntel*

cocoa der Kakao *kak_o_w*

coconut die Kokosnuß *k_o_kos-nooss*

cod der Kabeljau *k_a_belyow*

coffee der Kaffee *k_a_ffay*; **with sugar** mit Zucker *mìt tsookker*; **with milk** mit Milch *mìt mìlsh*; **decaffeinated** entkoffeinierter Kaffee *ent koffigh_nee_erter k_a_ffay*

coin die Münze *m_o_ontse*

cold cuts Wurstwaren *voorst-v_a_ren*

cold kalt *kalt*

Cologne Köln *kerln*

color die Farbe *farbe*

come, to kommen *kommen*

comfortable bequem *bekvem*

comforter der Schnuller *shnooller*

complaint die Beschwerde *beshverde*

compulsory verpflichtend *ferpflishtent*

cone der Kegel *kegel*, die Eistüte *ighs-toote*

confectionery die Süßwaren *soossvaaren*

confirm, to bestätigen *beshtètigen*

contact lenses die Kontaktlinsen *kontaktlinsen*

contents der Inhalt *inhalt*

continue, to weitermachen *vightermakhen*, fortfahren *fortfaaren*

control, to kontrollieren *kontrolleeren*

cook (m) der Koch *kokh* **cook (f)** die Köchin *kershin*

cook, to kochen *kokhen*, garen *gaaren*

cooking der Kochvorgang *kokh-forgang*, die Kochzeit *kokh-tsight*

cork der Korken *korken*

corn der Mais *mighs*

corncob der Maiskolben *mighskolben*

corner die Ecke *èkhe*

cost der Preis *prighs*, die Kosten *kosten*

cost, to kosten *kosten*

cottage cheese der Quark *kvaark*

cotton die Baumwolle *bowmvolle*

country das Land *lant*

countryside (auf dem) Land *(owf dem) lant*

courgettes die Zucchini *tsookeenee*

cover das Gedeck *gedèk*

cover, to bedecken *bedèkken*

crab der Krebs *kreps*

cracker das Hähnchen *hènshen*

crackers das Salzgebäck *salts-gebèk*

cranberries Preiselbeeren *prighselbayeren*

cream die Creme *krem*, die Sahne *saane*; **whipped cream** die Schlagsahne *shlak-saane*

cream puff der Windbeutel *vint-boytel*

credit card die Kreditkarte *kredeet-karte*

croissant das Hörnchen *hernshen*

croquette die Kroketten *krochètten*

crowded überfüllt *ooberfoolt*

cruet das Ölkännchen *erl-kènshen*

crunchy knusprig *knoosprik*

crust die Kruste *krooste*

cube der Würfel *voorfel*; **ice cube** der Eiswürfel *ighsvoorfel*

cucumber die Salatgurke *salat-gurke*

cumin der Kümmel *koommel*

cup die Tasse *tasse*

currant die Johannisbeere *yohannis-bayere*

currency Wert *vert*, die Währung *vèroong*

cushion das Kissen *kissen*

cut, to schneiden *shnighden*

cutlery das Besteck *beshtek*

cutlet das Kotelett *kottlett*, das Schnitzel *shnitzel*

damp feucht *foysht*

dance, to tanzen *tantsen*

dark dunkel *doonkel*

dates die Datteln *datteln*

daughter die Tochter *tokhte*

day der Tag *tak*

dear lieb *leep*, teuer *toyer*

debit, to berechnen *berèshnen*, in Rechnung stellen *in rèshnoongh shtèllen*

December der Dezember *detsèmber*

decorated dekoriert *dekoreert*, geschmückt *geshmookt*

decoration die Verzierung *fertseeroong*, die Dekoration *dekoratseeon*

delay die Verspätung *ferspetoongh*

dentist der Zahnarzt *tsaan-artst*

dentures das Gebiß *gebiss*, die dritten Zähne *dee dritten tsène*

deposit, to hinterlegen *hinterlegen*, zur Aufbewahrung geben *tsoor owfbevaaroong geben*

dessert der Nachtisch _naakhtish_

diabetic zuckerkrank _zookker-krànk_, der Diabetiker _deeabetiker_

diet die Diät _dee-èt_, die Ernährung _ernèroong_

different anders _anders_, verschieden _fersheeden_

difficult schwierig _shveerik_

digestible verdaulich _ferdowlish_

dinner das Abendessen _abent-èssen_

dirt der Schmutz _shmootz_

dirty schmutzig _shmootsik_

disabled behindert _behindert_

disco die Diskothek _diskotek_

dish das Gericht _gerisht_

disinfectant desinfizierend _desinfitseerent_, der Desinfizierer _desinfitseerer_

distance die Entfernung _entfèrnoong_

disturb, to stören _shter-ren_

do, to tun _toon_, machen _makhen_

doctor der Arzt _arzt_, Doktor _doktor_

documents die Dokumente _dokoomènte_, die Papiere _papeere_

donut der Krapfen _krapfen_, Berliner _berliner_

door die Tür _toor_

double doppelt _doppelt_, das Doppelte _doppelte_

dough der Teig _tighk_; **(leavened pastry)** der Hefeteig _hayfe-tighk_

down unten _oonten_, unter _oonter_

draft vom Faß _fom fass_

draught der Luftzug _looft-tsoog_, laufend _lowfent_

drink das Getränk _getrènk_

drink, to trinken _trinken_

dry trocken _trokken_

duck die Ente _ènte_

dummy der Schnuller _shnooller_

Dutch holländisch _hollèndish_

duty die Pflicht _pflisht_,

earring der Ohrring _oring_

Easter Ostern _ostern_

easy einfach _ighnfach_

eat, to essen _èssen_

economic preiswert _prighsvert_

eel der Aal _àal_

egg das Ei *igh*; **boiled eggs**
gekochte Eier *gek_okhte_
_igher_*; **scrambled eggs**
Rühreier *roorigher*; **fried
eggs** Spiegeleier *shpeegel-
igher*

eggplant die Aubergine
obersheenen

egg white das Eiweiß
ighvighs

elevator der Aufzug
owftsppg

embassy die Botschaft
botshaft

empty leer *layer*

end das Ende *ènde*

endive die Endivie
endeeveeay

England England *ènglant*

English englisch *ènglish*, der
Engländer *ènglènder*

enough genügend *gen_oo_gent*

enter, to eintreten
ighntreten, hineingehen
hin_igh_ngayhen

entrance der Eingang
ighngang

error der Irrtum *irrtoom*, der
Fehler *fayler*

escalope das Schnitzel
shnitsel

evening der Abend *_aa_bent*

every jeder *y_ay_der*

except außer *owsser*

exchange der Wechsel(kurs)
vèxel-(koors), die
Änderung *ènderoong*

excursion der Ausflug
owsfluk

exit der Ausgang *owsgang*

expense die Ausgabe
owsgabe

expensive teuer *toyer*

expert der Experte *expèrte*

expresso der Espressokaffee
esprèsso-kaffay

extract der Extrakt *extr_a_kt*,
der Auszug *owstsoog*

eye das Auge *owge*

fainted ohnmächtig
onmèshtik

fall, to fallen *f_a_len*

familiar bekannt *bek_a_nnt*,
vertraut *fertrowt*

family die Familie *fam_i_lee*

famous berühmt *ber_oo_mt*

far weit *vight*

farm die Zucht *ts_oo_kht*

fat fett *fèt*, das Fett *fèt*

fatty fettig *fettik*

favor der Gefallen *gef_a_len*

feast day das Fest *fèst*

February der Februar *febrooar*

feel, to fühlen *foolen*

feet die Füße *foosse*; **on foot** zu Fuß *tsoo fooss*

fennel der Fenchel *fènshel*

fig die Feige *figh-ge*

fillet das Filet *fillay*

filling die Füllung *foolloongh*

filter, to filtern *filtern*

find, to finden *finden*

fine fein *fighn*

finish, to beenden *bayènden*

fire das Feuer *foyer*

fish der Fisch *fish*

fishing das Angeln *angeln*

flame die Flamme *flamme*

flat platt *plat*

flavor der Geschmack *geshmak*

flavor, to würzen *voorzen*

flavored schmackhaft *shmakhaft*, würzig *voortsik*

flesh (of fruit) das Fruchtfleisch *frookht-flighsh*

flight der Flug *fluk*

floor (story) das Stockwerk *shtokvèrk*

flour das Mehl *mayl*

flowers die Blumen *bloomen*

fly die Fliege *fleege*

fondue das Fondue *fondoo*

food colorings die Farbstoffe *farb-shtoffe*

food poisoning die Lebensmittelvergiftung *laybensmittel-fergiftoong*

foodstuffs die Lebensmittel *laybens-mittel*

for für *foor*, nach *nakh*

foreigner der Fremde *fremde*, der Ausländer *owslènder*

forget, to vergessen *fergèssen*

fork die Gabel *gaabel*

France Frankreich *frankrighsh*

Franconia Franken *franken*

Frankfurt Frankfurt *frankfoort*

frankfurter die Wurst *voorst*, das Würstchen *voorst-shen*, Würstel *voorstel*

free gratis _gratis_, frei _frigh_

French französisch
frantsersish

fresh frisch _frìsh_

freshly squeezed juice frisch
ausgepreßter Saft _frish
owsgepresster saft_

Friday Freitag _frightak_

fried gebraten _gebraten_,
fritiert _friteert_

friend (m) der Freund
froynd; **friend (f)** die
Freundin _froyndin_

frozen gefroren _gefroren_

fruit das Obst _opst_; **fresh
fruit** frisches Obst _frishes
opst_; **dried fruit**
Trockenobst _trokken-opst_;
wild berries die
Waldfrüchte _valt-frooshte_

fruit salad der Obstsalat
opst-salaat

frying pan die Pfanne _pfanne_

full voll _foll_; **full-bodied**
vollmundig _follmoondeeg_

game das Wild(bret)
vilt(bret); **game (meat)** das
Wild(bret) _vilt-(bret)_

garden der Garten _garten_

garlic der Knoblauch
knoblowkh

garnish die Verzierung
fertseeroong

gasoline pump die
Tankstelle _tankshtèlle_

gelatine das Gelee _shelay_,
der Aspik _aspik_

German deutsch _doytsh_,
Deutscher _doytsher_

Germany Deutschland
doytsh-lant

gherkins die Gewürzgurke
gevoorts-goorke

ginger der Ingwer _ingver_

girl das Mädchen _mèdshen_

give, to geben _geben_

glass das Glas _glaas_; **small
glass** das Gläschen _glès-
shen_

gloves die Handschuhe
hantshoohe

go, to gehen _gehen_

goat die Ziege _tseege_

gold das Gold _golt_

golden vergoldet _fergoldet_,
goldgelb _gold-gèlp_

good gut _goot_

goose die Gans _gans_

go out, to hinausgehen
hinows-gayhen

go up, to aufsteigen
owfshtighgen, einsteigen
ighnshtighgen

grain der Weizen *vightsen*, das Korn *korn*

grape die Traube *trowbe*

grapefruit die Pampelmuse *pampelmoose*, Grapefruit *graypfroot*

grated gerieben *gereeben*

greasy fettig *fettik*

Greece Griechenland *greeshen-lant*

Greek griechisch *greeshish*

green beans grüne Bohnen *groone bonen*

green grün *groon*

grill der Grill *grill*, das Rost *rost*

grilled vom Grill *fom grill*

ground meat das Hackfleisch *hakflighsh*

group die Gruppe *grooppe*; **group leader** der Gruppenleiter *grooppen-lighter*

guard die Wache *vakhe*, der Wächter *vèshter*

guard, to bewachen *bevakhen*

guide der (Reise)Führer *(righse)foorer*

guinea fowl das Perlhuhn *pèrl-hoon*

hake der Seehecht *saye-hèsht*

half die Hälfte *hèlfte*

half halb *halp*

ham (cooked) gekochter Schinken *gekokhter shinken*; **ham (cured)** roher Schinken *roher shinken*

Hamburg Hamburg *hamboorg*

hand die Hand *hant*

handbag die Handtasche *hant-tashe*

happen, to passieren *passeeren*

happy glücklich *glook-lish*, zufrieden *tsoofreeden*

hard hart *haart*, fest *fest*

hare der Hase *haase*

harmless unschädlich *oon-shèdlish*

hat der Hut *hoot*

have, to haben *haaben*

hazelnut die Haselnüsse *haasel-noosse*

headache die Kopfschmerzen *kopf-shmèrtsen*

health die Gesundheit *gesoont-hight*

hear, to hören _her-ren_

heat, to erwärmen _ervèrmen_, heizen _hightsen_

heating die Heizung _hightsoong_

heavy schwer _shver_

help Hilfe _hilfe_

help, to helfen _hèlfen_

hen das Huhn _hoon_

herbs die Kräuter _kroyter_

here hier _heer_

herring der Hering _hereeng_

highchair der Hochstuhl (für Kinder) _hokh-shtool foor kinder_

hiring die Vermietung _vermeetoong_

hold, to halten _halten_, haben _haaben_

holiday der Feiertag _fighertak_

holidays die Ferien _fereen_, der Urlaub _oorlowp_

Holland Holland _hollant_

homogenized homogenisiert _homogayniseert_

hospital das Krankenhaus _kranken-hows_

hot heiß _highs_

hotel das Hotel _hotel_

hour die Stunde _shtoonde_

house das Haus _hows_

how much/many wieviel _vifeel_

how wie _vee_

hundred hundert _hoondert_

hunger der Hunger _hoonger_

hurry die Eile _ighle_

husband der Ehemann _ayheman_

ice das Eis _ighs_; **ice cream** das Eis _ighs_; **ice cream parlour** die Eisdiele _ighs-deele_

icing der Zuckerguß _tsookker-gooss_

identity card der Personalausweis _personal-owsvighs_

ill krank _krank_

immediately sofort _sofort_

important wichtig _vishtik_

impossible unmöglich _oonmerglish_

in front of vor _foor_, davor _dafoor_

included inbegriffen _inbegriffen_

inform, to informieren _informeeren_

information die Information *informatseeon*

infusion der Kräutertee *kroytertay*

inn das Gasthaus *gasthows*

insect das Insekt *insèkt*

inside innen *innen*, Innen *innen*; drinnen *drinnen*

instead anstatt *anshtat*

instruction der Hinweis *hinvighs*

interior innerlich *innerlish*

invite, to einladen *ighnlaaden*

invoice die Rechnung *rèshnoong*, die Anfertigung *anferti-goong*

Italian italienisch *italeeaynish*, der/die Italiener/in *italeeayner/in*

Italy Italien *italien*

jacket die/das Jacke(tt) *yakke, jakkètt*

jam die Konfitüre *kon-fitoore*

January Januar *yanooar*

juice der Saft *saft*; **fruit juice** der Obstsaft *opstsaft*

July Juli *yoolee*

June Juni *yoonee*

juniper der Wacholder *vakholder*

just allein *allighn*, nur *noor*

kidneys die Niere *neere*

kitchen die Küche *kooshe*

kiwi fruit die Kiwi *keevee*

knife das Messer *mèsser*

know, to wissen *vissen*, kennen *kennen*

label das Etikett *etikett*

lady Dame *daame*

lager Helles *hèlles*

lake der See *say*

lamb das Lamm *lam*

lard das Schmalz *shmalts*, der Speck *shpèk*

large groß *gross*, kräftig *krèftish*

last letzter *letster*

lay the table, to (den Tisch) decken *(den tìsh) dèkken*

leave, to abreisen *aprighsen*, lassen *lassen*

leeks der Porree *porray*

leg das Bein *bighn*

lemon die Zitrone *zitrone*

lemonade die Zitronenlimonade *zitronen-leemonaade*

lentils die Linsen *linsen*

less weniger *vayniger*

lettuce der Kopfsalat *kopf-salaat*

light das Licht *lisht*

light leicht *lighsht*

light, to anzünden *antsoonden*, anstellen *anshtellen*

like, to mögen *mergen*

line die Linie *leeniay*, die Leitung *lightungh*

liquer der Schnaps *shnaps*

liquidise, to quirlen *kvayrlen*

liquor der Likör *liker*

list das Verzeichnis *fertsighshnis*, die Liste *liste*

lit angezündet *angetsoondet*

liter der Liter *leeter*

little klein *klighn*, wenig *vaynik*

liver die Leber *layber*

lobster der Hummer *hoommer*

local örtlich *errtlish*

loin das Lendenstück *lènden-shtook*

long lang *lang*; **long-distance call** das Ferngespräch *fèrn-geshprèèsh*

lose, to verlieren *ferleeren*

lozenge die Tablette *tablètte*

lunch das Mittagessen *mittak-essen*

mackerel die Makrele *makrele*

macrobiotic makrobiotisch *macro-beeotish*

main course die Hauptspeise *howpt-shpighse*

make, to tun *toon*, machen *makhen*

manager der Direktor *deerèktor*

mandarin die Mandarine *mandareene*

map die Karte *karte*

March März *mèrts*

marinated die Marinade *mareenaade*

market der Markt *maarkt*

marmelade die Marmelade *marmelaade*

match das Streichholz *shtrighsh-holts*

matter die Sache *sakhe*, was *vas*

mature reif *righf*

matured abgehangen *abgehangen*, gereift *gerighft*

May Mai *migh*

mayonnaise die Mayonnaise *mighon<u>ay</u>say*

meal die Mahlzeit *m<u>aa</u>ltsight*

mean, to bedeuten *bed<u>oy</u>ten*

medicine die Medizin *medits<u>ee</u>n*

meet, to treffen *tr<u>è</u>ffen*

melon die Honigmelone *h<u>o</u>nik-mel<u>o</u>ne*

menu das Menü *men<u>oo</u>,* die Speisekarte *shp<u>igh</u>se-k<u>a</u>rte*

meringue das Baiser *bès<u>ay</u>*

Milan Mailand *m<u>igh</u>lant*

milk die Milch *milsh*

milkshake der Milchshake *milsh-sh<u>igh</u>k*

minestrone der Gemüseeintopf *gem<u>oo</u>se-<u>igh</u>ntopf*

mint die Pfefferminze *pf<u>e</u>fferminze*

minute die Minute *min<u>oo</u>te*

mistake der Fehler *f<u>ay</u>ler,* Irrtum *<u>ee</u>rtoom*

misunderstood das Mißverständnis *miss-ferst<u>è</u>ndnis*

mixed gemischt *gem<u>i</u>sht*

Monday Montag *m<u>o</u>ntak*

month der Monat *m<u>o</u>nat*

monument das Denkmal *d<u>è</u>nkmaal*

more mehr *mayer*

morning der Morgen *m<u>o</u>rgen*

Moselle die Mosel *m<u>o</u>sel*

mosquito die Mücken *m<u>oo</u>kken*

mother die Mutter *m<u>oo</u>tter*

mouth der Mund *moont*

Mr. der Herr *hèrr*

Mrs. die Frau *frow*

Munich München *m<u>oo</u>nshen*

museum das Museum *moos<u>ay</u>oom*

mushrooms die Pilze *p<u>i</u>ltse*

music die Musik *moos<u>ee</u>k*

mussels die Miesmuscheln *m<u>ee</u>s-m<u>oo</u>sheln*

must (have to) müssen *m<u>oo</u>ssen*

mustard der Senf *senf*

mutton der Hammel *h<u>a</u>mmel*

name der Name *n<u>aa</u>me*

napkin die Serviette *servee-<u>e</u>tte*

narrow eng *eng*

nearly fast *fast,* beinahe *b<u>igh</u>naahe*

need das Bedürfnis *bed<u>oo</u>rfnis,* der Bedarf *bed<u>a</u>rf*

need, to brauchen *br<u>ow</u>khen*
never nie *nee*
New Year Neujahr *n<u>oy</u> -yaar*
newspaper die Zeitung *t<u>aigh</u>toong*
next to neben *n<u>ay</u>ben*
noise der Krach *krakh*, Lärm *lèrm*
noisy laut *lowt*, geräuschvoll *ger<u>oy</u>shfol*
non-alcoholic alkoholfrei *alkoh<u>o</u>l-frigh*
non-smoking der Nichtraucher *nisht-r<u>ow</u>kher*
noodles die Nudeln *n<u>oo</u>deln*
no-one keiner *k<u>igh</u>ner*
north der Norden *n<u>o</u>rden*
nothing nichts *nishts*
nougat das Nougat *n<u>oo</u>gat*
November November *nov<u>è</u>mber*
number die Zahl *tsaal*, Nummer *n<u>oo</u>mmer*
nutcracker der Nußknacker *nooss-kn<u>a</u>kker*
nutmeg die Muskatnuß *musk<u>aa</u>t-nooss*

oats der Hafer *h<u>aa</u>fer*
obtain, to erhalten *erh<u>a</u>lten*
October Oktober *okt<u>o</u>ber*

offal die Innereien *inner<u>igh</u>en*
often häufig *h<u>oy</u>fik*, oft *oft*
oil das Öl *erl*
oily ölig *<u>er</u>lik*
olives die Oliven *ol<u>ee</u>ven*
omelet das Omelett *oml<u>è</u>tt*
on an *an*
onion die Zwiebel *tsv<u>ee</u>bel*
only nur *noor*
open offen *<u>o</u>ffen*, auf *owf*
orange die Apfelsine *apfels<u>ee</u>ne*
orangeade die Orangenlimonade *or<u>o</u>ngen-leemon<u>a</u>de*
order die Bestellung *besht<u>è</u>lloong*
order, to bestellen *besht<u>è</u>llen*
oregano das Oregano *or<u>e</u>gano*
other anderes *<u>a</u>nderes*, noch etwas *nokh ètvas*
outing der Ausflug *<u>ow</u>sflook*
outside äußerlich *<u>oy</u>sserlish*, Außen-*<u>ow</u>ssen*, draußen *dr<u>ow</u>ssen*
oven der Ofen *<u>o</u>fen*
own eigen *<u>igh</u>gen*
ox der Ochse *<u>o</u>xe*
oyster die Austern *<u>ow</u>stern*

pacifier der Schnuller *shnooller*

packaged abgepackt *ab-gepackt*

pair das Paar, paar *par*

pan die Feder *fayder*

paper bag die Tüte *toote*

parents die Eltern *èltern*

park der Park *park*

parsley die Petersilie *petersilee*

part der Teil *tighl*

passport der Reisepaß *righse-pass*

pasta twists die Zöpfli *zerpfli*

pastries die Mürbeteigkekse *moorbetighg-kekse*, die Teilchen *tighlshen*

pay, to zahlen *tsaalen*

payment die Zahlung *tsaaloong*

peach der Pfirsich *pfirsish*

peanut die Erdnuß *erdnooss*

pear die Birne *beerne*

peas die Erbsen *èrpsen*

peel, to pellen *pèllen*, schälen *shelen*

pencil der Bleistift *blighshtift*

pepper der Pfeffer *pfèffer*

peppermill die Pfeffermühle *pfèffer-moole*

perch der Barsch *barsh*

perhaps vielleicht *fillighsht*

permit die Erlaubnis *erlowbnis*

pharmacy die Apotheke *apotayke*

pheasant der Fasan *fasaan*

photograph das Foto *foto*

pickles (in oil) in Öl Eingelegtes *in ool ighngelaygtes*; **(in vinegar)** in Essig Eingelegtes *in èssik ine-gelaygtes*

piece das Stück *shtook*

pig das Schwein *shvighn*

pigeon die Taube *towbe*

pike der Hecht *hesht*

pill die Pille *pille*

pineapple die Ananas *ananas*

pine kernel die Pinienkerne *pineen-kèrne*

pistacchios die Pistazien *pistatseen*

place der (Sitz)platz *(sits)-plats*, der Ort *ort*

plant die Pflanze *pflantse*

plate der Teller *tèller*

play, to spielen *shpeelen*

please bitte *bitte*

please (like), to gefallen *gefallen*,

pleasure das Gefallen *gefallen*, das Vergnügen *fergnoogen*

plum die Pflaume *pflowme*

popsicle das Wassereis *vasser-ighs*

porcini mushrooms die Steinpilze *shtighn-piltse*

pork das Schwein *shvighn*

portion die Portion *portseeon*

possible möglich *merglish*

postage stamp die Briefmarke *breef-marke*

postcard die Postkarte *postkarte*

potatoes die Kartoffeln *kartoffeln*; **French fries** die Pommes frites *pom-frits*; **boiled potatoes** die Pellkartoffeln *pèll-kartoffeln*

prawns die Krabben *krabben*, die Garnelen *garnaylen*

prefer, to vorziehen *fortseehen*, bevorzugen *befortsoogen*

pregnant schwanger *shvanger*

prepare, to vorbereiten *forberighten*, zubereiten *zooberighten*

preservatives die Konservierungsstoffe *konserveeroongs-shtoffe*

preserved eingemacht *ighnge-makht*

price der Preis *prighs*

pudding der Pudding *poodding*

puff pastry der Blätterteig *blètter-tighk*

pulses die Hülsenfrüchte *hoolsenfrooshte*

pumpkin der Kürbis *koorbis*

purée das Püree *pooray*

put, to setzen *sètsen*, stellen *shtèllen*, legen *laygen*

quarter das Viertel *feertel*

question die Frage *fraage*

quiche die Wähe *vèhe*, Quiche *kish*

quick schnell *shnell*

quil die Wachtel *vakhtel*

quite ziemlich *zeemlish*

rabbit das Kaninchen *kaninshen*

radio das Radio *radeeo*

radish die Radieschen *radees-shen*

raincoat der Regenmantel *regen-mantel*

aisin die Rosine *roseene*

are (meat) englisch *english*

aspberries die Himbeeren *himbayren*

aw roh *ro*

ead, to lesen *laysen*

eady fertig *fèrtik*

eceipt die Quittung *kvittoong*

ecipe das Rezept *retsept*

efrigerator der Kühlschrank *koolshrank*

efund die Vergütung *fergootoongh*, Erstattung *erstattoongh*

egion die Region *regeeon*

emain, to bleiben *blighben*

emove the fat from, to entfetten *entfetten*

emove, to wegnehmen *veknaymen*

eply, to antworten *antvorten*

eservation die Reservierung *reserveeroong*

eserve, to reservieren *reserveeren*

eserved reserviert *reserveert*

est der Rest *rest*

estaurant das Restaurant *restorong*

restroom die Toilette *tolètte*, das Bad *baat*

return die Rückkehr *rookkayer*

return, to zurückkommen *tsoorook-kommen*

Rhine der Rhein *righn*

rice der Reis *righs*

right richtig *rèkhte*; **to the right** rechts *rèkhts*

ripe reif *righf*

road die Straße *shtraasse*

roast gebraten *gebraten*, der Braten *braten*; **roast suckling pig** das Spanferkel *shpan-fèrkel*

roast, to gebraten *gebraten*, geröstet *gererstet*

roasted geröstet *geruustet*

rocket die Rauke *rowke*

Rome Rom *rom*

room der Saal *saal*, die Halle *halle*, das Zimmer *tsimmer*

rosemary der Rosmarin *rosmarin*

roulades die Rouladen *roolaaden*

rustic rustikal *roostikaal*

safety pin die Sicherheitsnadel *sisherhights-naadel*

saffron der Safran _safran_
sage der Salbei _salbigh_
salad der Salat _salaat_
salami die Salami _salaami_
Salmon der Lachs _lax_;
  smoked salmon der
  Räucherlachs _roysher-lax_
salt das Salz _salts_; **saltcellar**
  der Salzstreuer _salts-shtroyer_
salty salzig _saltsik_
Salzburg Salzburg _saltsboork_
same (der)selbe _(der)selbe_,
  egal _egaal_, gleich _glighsh_
sardines die Sardinen
  sardeenen
Saturday Samstag _samstak_
sauce die (Tomaten-)Soße
  (tom_aa_ten-)_sosse_
saucepan der Topf _topf_
sausage die Wurst _voorst_,
  das Würstchen _voorstshen_
sausages die Wurstwaren
  voorst-vaaren
Savoy cabbage der Wirsing
  veersing
say, to sagen _saagen_
scampi die Garnelen
  garnaylen
sea das Meer _mayer_
season die Jahreszeit
  yaarestsight

seasoning die Würze _voorze_
  das Gewürz _ghevoorts_
second (2nd) zweiter Gang
  tsvighter gang
see, to sehen _sayn_
sell, to verkaufen _ferkowfen_
semolina der Grieß _greess_
September September _september_
service die Bedienung
  bedeenoong
shank die Haxe _haxe_
shell die Schale _shaale_, die
  Hülse _hoolse_
shell, to schälen _shèlen_
shellfish die Weichtiere
  vighsh-teere, Schalentiere
  shaalen-teere
shirt das Hemd _hèmt_
shoots die Sprossen
  shprossen
shop das Geschäft _geshèft_
shopping der Einkauf
  ighnkowf; **shopping cart**
  Einkaufswagen _ighnkowfs-vagen_
shortcrust pastry der
  Mürbeteig _moorbe-tighk_
shoulder die Schulter
  shoolter
show die Vorstellung
  vorshtelloong

how, to zeigen *tsighgen*

ide dish die Beilage *bighlage*

ign die Bezeichnung *bezaishnungh*

ignature die Unterschrift *untershrift*

imple einfach *ighnfakh*

killet die Pfanne *pfanne*, flacher Kochtopf *flakher kokh-topf*

lice die Scheibe *shighbe*

liced bread das Toastbrot *tostbroot*

liced der Aufschnitt *owfshnitt*

mell der Geruch *gerookh*

mell, to riechen *reeshen*

moke, to rauchen *rowkhen*

moked geräuchert *geroyshert*

moker der Raucher *rowkher*

nooth glatt *glat*

nack der Snack *snèk*, Imbiß *imbiss*; **snack bar** das Schnellrestaurant *shnell-restorong*, der Imbiß *imbiss*

nail die Schnecke *shnèkke*

oap die Seife *sighfe*

ole die Seezunge *saye-tsoonge*

ome einige *ighnige*

someone jemand *yemant*

something etwas *etvas*

son der Sohn *son*

song das Lied *leet*

sorbet das Sorbet *sorbay*, Fruchteis *frookht-ighs*

soufflé der Auflauf *owflowf*, die Pastete *pastete*

soup die Suppe *sooppe*

sour sauer *sower*, herb *hèrb*

south der Süden *sooden*

soya das Soja *soya*

sparkling sprudelnd *shproodelnt*

spectacles die Brille *brille*

spices die Gewürze *gevoortse*

spicy scharf *sharf*

spinach der Spinat *shpinaat*

spirits die Spirituosen *shpiritoo-osen*

spit der Spieß *shpeess*

sponge das Biskuit *biskvit*

spoon der (Eß)löffel *(èss)-lerffel*; **teaspoon** der Teelöffel *taylerffel*; **coffeespoon** der Kaffeelöffel *kaffelerffel*

square der Platz *plats*

squid die Tintenfische *tinten-fishe*

stair die Treppe *trèppe*

starch die Speisestärke *shpighse-shtèrke*

station der Bahnhof *baanhof*

stay, to bleiben *blighben*

steak das Steak *stayk*; **grilled steak** vom Grill *fom grìll*

steam der Dampf *dampf*

steamed gedünstet *gedoonstet*

stew geschmort *geshmort*, der Schmorbraten *shmorbraaten*, Auflauf *owf-lowf*; Geschnetzeltes *geshnètseltes*

sticking plaster das Pflaster *pflaster*

still noch *nokh*

stock cube der Würfel *voorfel*

stomach ache die Magenschmerzen *maagen-shmèrtsen*

stop, to anhalten *anhalten*

stopper Stopfen *shtopfen*

stout Dunkles *doonkles*

straight geradeaus *gerade-ows*, das Recht *rèsht*

strawberry die Erdbeere *èrtbayre*; **strawberries and cream** Erdbeeren mit Sahne *èrtbayren mìt saane*

street die Straße *shtraasse*

strong stark *shtark*

stuffed gefüllt *gefoollt*

subway die U-Bahn *oobaar*

sugar der Zucker *tsookker*; **sugar bowl** die Zuckerdose *tsookker-dos*

suitcase der Koffer *koffer*

summer der Sommer *sommer*

summery sommerlich *sommerlish*

Sunday der Sonntag *sonnta*

surname der Nachname *nakh-naame*

surroundings die Umgebun *umgeboong*

sweet süß *sooss*, die Süßspeise *sooss-shpighse* das Bonbon *bon-bon*

sweet-and-sour süß-sauer *sooss-sower*

sweetbread das Bries *brees*

sweetener der Süßstoff *sooss-shtoff*

swim, to schwimmen *shvimmen*

swimming pool das Schwimmbad *shvim-bat*

Switzerland die Schweiz *shvights*

syrup der Sirup *seeroop*

tabacconist's der Tabakwarenladen *tabak-vaaren-laaden*

table der Tisch *tish*; **tablecloth** die Tischdecke *tishdekke*

take, to nehmen *naymen*

talcum powder der Puder *pooder*

tart der Kuchen *cookhen*, die Pastete *pastete*

taste der Geschmack *geshmak*; die Kostprobe *kostprobe*

taste, to schmecken *shmèkken*

tea der Tee *tay*

telephone das Telefon *taylayfoon*; **telephone call** der Telefonanruf *taylayfon-anroof*; **telephone directory** das Telefonbuch *telefon-bookh*

temperature die Temperatur *temperatoor*; **room temperature** die Raumtemperatur *rowm-temperatoor*

tender zart *tsaart*

terrace die Terrasse *terasse*

terrine die Terrine *tereene*

thank you danke *danke*

thank, to bedanken *bedanken*

that jener *yayner*

then dann *dan*

thigh der Schenkel *shènkel*

thin dünn *doonn*

thirst der Durst *doorst*

this dieser *deeser*

this evening heute abend *hoyte aabent*

thousand tausend *towsent*

thread der Faden *faaden*

throat die Kehle *kayle*, der Hals *hals*

throw, to werfen *vèrfen*

Thursday Donnerstag *donners-tak*

thyme der Thymian *toomeean*

ticket die Fahrkarte *faarkarte*, Eintrittskarte *ighntritts-karte*

tie die Krawatte *kravatte*

tight eng *eng*

till die Kasse *kasse*

time die Zeit *tsight*

timetable der Fahrplan *faarplaan*

tip das Trinkgeld *trinkgelt*

toast der Trinkspruch *trink-shprookh*

toasted getoastet *getostet*

today heute *hoyte*

together zusammen *tsusammen*

tomato die Tomate *tomaate*

tomorrow morgen *morgen*

tongue die Zunge *tsoonge*

too much zu viel *tsoo feel*

tooth der Zahn *tsaan*; **toothpick** der Zahnstocher *tsaan-shtokher*

towards nach *naakh*

towel das Handtuch *hand-tookh*

train der Zug *tsook*

transport der Transport *transport*; **means of transport** das Transportmittel *transport-mittel*

tray das Tablett *tablètt*

tripe die Kutteln *kootteln*

trout die Forelle *forelle*

truffle der Trüffel *trooffel*

try, to probieren *probeeren*, kosten *kosten*

tuna der Thunfisch *toonfish*

turkey der Truthahn *troot-haan*

turn die Drehung *drehoong*, die Runde *roonde*

turn, to drehen *drayhen*, umrühren *oomrooren*

turnip die Rübe *roobe*

turn off, to ausschalten *ows-shalten*

type die Gattung *gattoong*, die Art *art*

ugly häßlich *hèsslish*

umbrella der Schirm *shirm*

uncomfortable unbequem *oonbekvaym*

uncork, to entkorken *entkorken*

under unter *oonter*

understand, to verstehen *fershtehen*

understood verstanden *fershtanden*, inbegriffen *inbe-griffen*

United States Vereinigte Staaten *verighnigte shtaaten*

unripe herb *hèrb*, unreif *oonrighf*

until bis *beess*

use, to benutzen *benootsen*

vacation die Ferien *fayree-en*, der Urlaub *urlowp*

vacuum-packed
vakuumverpackt *vakoom-ferpakt*

vanilla die Vanille *vanile*

V.A.T. die Mehrwertsteuer *mervert-shtoyer*

veal das Kalb *kalp*

vegetable garden der Gemüsegarten *gemoose-garten*

vegetables das (Garten-)gemüse *(garten-)gemoose*

vegetarian vegetarisch *vegetarish*, der Vegetarier *vegetareer*

very viel *feel*

via über *oober*

Vienna Wien *veen*

view die Sicht *sisht*, Aussicht *owssisht*

village Dorf *dorf*

vinegar der Essig *èssig*

vintage der Jahrgang *yargang*

vitamins die Vitamine *vitameene*

wait, to warten *varten*

waiter der Kellner *kèllner*; **waitress** die Kellnerin *kèllnerin*

walk, to (spazieren)gehen *(shpatseeren)-gehen*

wall die Mauer *mower*

wallet die Brieftasche *breeftashe*

walnut die Walnuß *val-nooss*

want, to wünschen *voonshen*, wollen *vollen*

wardrobe die Garderobe *garderobe*

warn, to warnen *varnen*, verständigen *fershtèndeegen*

wash, to waschen *vashen*

wasp die Wespe *vespe*

watch die Uhr *oor*

watch, to schauen *showen*

water das Wasser *vasser*; **mineral water** das Mineralwasser *meenayralvasser*; **still** ohne Kohlensäure *one kolen-soyre*; **sparkling** mit Kohlensäure *mit kolen-soyre*

watermelon die Wassermelone *vasser-melone*

waterproof wasserundurchlässig *vasser-oondoorsh-lèssig*

weak schwach *shvakh*

weather das Wetter *vetter*

Wednesday Mittwoch *mitvokh*

week die Woche *vokhe*

weekday der Wochentag *vokhen-tak*

welcome willkommen *villkommen*

welcome, you're bitte *bitte*

What? was? *vas*

when wann *van*

where wo *vo*

which welche *velshe*

while während *vèrent*

white weiß *vighs*

Who? wer? *ver*

whole ganz *gants*

wholemeal vollständig *foll-shtèndik*, Vollkorn- *follkorn*

wife die Ehefrau *ayhefrow*

window das Fenster *fènster*

wine der Wein *vighn*; **white wine** der Weißwein *vighss-vighn*; **red wine** der Rotwein *rot-vighn*; **sparkling wine** der Sekt *sekt*

wine tasting die Weinprobe *vighnprobe*

winter der Winter *vinter*

with mit *mit*

without ohne *one*

woman die Frau *frow*

word das Wort *vort*

work die Arbeit *arbight*

work, to funktionieren *foonk-tseeoneeren*, in Betrieb sein *in betreep sighn*

write, to schreiben *shrighben*

year das Jahr *yar*

yeast die Hefe *hayfe*

yellow gelb *gelp*

yesterday gestern *gèstern*

yet noch *nokh*

young jung *yoong*

zucchini die Zucchini *tsookeenee*

Zurich Zürich *tsoorikh* (Swiss pronunciation), *tsoorish* (German pronunciation)

Aal eel
Aalsuppe see 'Regional Dishes' p. 64
Äbbelwoisuppe see 'Regional Dishes' p. 61
Abend evening
Abendbrot, Abendessen dinner, see also 'Introduction' p. 5
aber but
Abfall garbage
abkühlen to cool
absagen to cancel
Abschluß conclusion
Absicht intention
Adresse address
Alkohol alcohol; **alkoholfrei** non-alcoholic; **alkoholisch** alcoholic; **alkoholische Getränke** alcoholic drinks
Allergie allergy
alles all
Alsterwasser see 'Drinks' p. 26
alt old
Alt(bier) see 'Drinks' p. 20
Alter age
Ananas pineapple; **Ananassaft** pineapple juice
andere(r) other(s)
anders different

Anfang beginning; **anfangen** to begin, to start
angebrannt burnt
Angeln to fish
anhalten to stop
Anis aniseed
ankommen to arrive
anrufen to call, to telephone
anschreiben to put on the bill
Antibiotikum antibiotic
antworten to reply
anziehen, sich to get dressed
anzünden to light
Aperitif aperitif
Apfel apple
Apfel-Blutwurst-Küchlein see 'Regional Dishes' p. 70
Apfelkompott, Apfelkraut, Apfelmus apple sauce, see 'Gastronomic Terms' p. 38 and 'Sweets, Cakes and Pastries' p. 29
Apfelkuchen see 'Sweets, Cakes and Pastries' p. 29
Apfelsaft apple juice
Apfelsaftschorle, Apfelschorle see 'Drinks' p. 26
Apfelsine orange
Apfelstrudel see 'Sweets, Cakes and Pastries' p. 29

Apotheke pharmacy, chemist's
Appenzeller see 'Cheeses' p. 17
Appetit appetite; **Guten Appetit** Bon appétit
Aprikose apricot
April April
Arbeit work; **arbeiten** to work
Arme Ritter see 'Sweets, Cakes and Pastries' p. 29
Aroma aroma; **aromatisch** aromatic
Art style
Artischocke artichoke; **Artischockenherzen** artichoke hearts
Arzt doctor
Asche ash; **Aschenbecher** ashtray
Aspirin aspirin
Aubergine eggplant
auch also
auf open
Aufguß infusion
Auflauf soufflé, see 'Gastronomic Terms' p. 38
aufmerksam careful
aufschneiden to slice
Aufschnitt cold cuts, see 'Gastronomic Terms' p. 38
Aufzug elevator

Auge eye
August August
Ausflug excursion
Ausgang exit
Ausland abroad; **Ausländer** foreigner
Ausrüstung equipment
ausrutschen to slide
äußerlich external
Auster oyster
ausverkauft sold
Auszogne see 'Sweets, Cakes and Pastries' p. 29
Avokado avocado

backen to bake
Bäckerei bakery
Backhendl see 'National Dishes' p. 43
Bad bath
Bahnhof station
Baiser meringue
bald soon
Banane banana
Bank bank
Banknote banknote
Bar bar, nightclub, see 'Where to Eat' p. 8
Bargeld cash
Barsch perch
Basel Basle

Basilikum basil

Basler Lummelbraten see 'National Dishes' p. 56

Bauchschmerzen stomach ache

Bauchstecherla see 'National Dishes' p. 46

Bauernbrot homemade bread

Bauernhof farm

Baumwolle cotton

Bayern Bavaria

bayerisch Bavarian

Bayerische Creme Bavarian cream, see 'Sweets, Cakes and Pastries' p. 29 and 'Recipes' p. 75

Béchamelkartoffeln see 'National Dishes' p. 46

Béchamelsoße bechamel sauce

bedecken to cover

Bedeutung meaning

Bedienung service; waiter, waitress

Bedürfnis need

beenden to finish

Beere berry

behalten to keep

behindert handicapped, disabled;
Behinderteneingang disabled entrance;

Behindertentoilette disabled toilet

Beilage side dish

Bein leg

Beinfleisch see 'National Dishes' p. 43

Beisel see 'Where to Eat' p. 8

bekommen to receive, to get

bekömmlich wholesome

belasten to charge

Belegtes Brot see 'Gastronomic Terms' p. 38

benutzen to use

bequem comfortable, convenient, easy

Berlin Berlin

Berliner (Pfannkuchen) see 'Sweets, Cakes and Pastries' p. 30

Berliner Weiße see 'Drinks' p. 23

Bern Berne

Berner Ratsherrenplatte, B. Rösti see 'National Dishes' p. 56, 57

beruhigend calming

Beruhigungsmittel sedative

berühmt famous

Beschwerde complaint

besetzt occupied

besser better

bestätigen confirm
Besteck cutlery
bestellen to order; **Bestellung** order
beste(r) best
Bete, rote beetroot
betreten to enter
Beuscherl see 'National Dishes' p. 43
bewachen to guard
Bewerbung application
Biene bee
Bienenstich see 'Sweets, Cakes and Pastries' p. 30
Bier beer **Bier vom Faß** draft beer
Biergarten, Bierhaus, Bierkeller pub, see also 'Where to Eat' p. 11
Bierschinken, Bierwurst see 'Sausages and Cold Cuts' p. 13
Biersuppe see 'Regional Dishes' p. 65
billig economic, cheap
Bircher Müsli see 'National Dishes' p. 57
Birne pear
Birne Helène see 'Sweets, Cakes and Pastries' p. 30
bis until
Biskuit sponge cake

Biskuitrolle see 'Sweets, Cakes and Pastries' p. 30
Bismarckhering marinated herring fillets, see also 'National Dishes' p. 46
Biß bite
Bistrot see 'Where to Eat' p. 8
bitte please, here you are
bitter bitter
blaß pale
Blätterteig puff pastry
Blau blue; see also 'Gastronomic Terms' p. 38
Blaue Zipfel see 'Regional Dishes' p. 65
Blaukraut red cabbage, see also 'National Dishes' p. 46
bleiben to remain, to stay
bleifrei lead free
Bleistift pencil
Blockwurst see 'Sausages and Cold Cuts' p. 13
Blumen flowers
Blumenkohl cauliflower
Bluse blouse
Blut blood
Blutwurst see 'Sausages and Cold Cuts' p. 13
Bock(bier) see 'Drinks' p. 20
Bœuf 'Stroganoff' see 'National Dishes' p. 46

Böfflamott see 'Regional Dishes' p. 65

Bohnen beans

Bonbon sweet, candy

böse bad

Botschaft embassy

Bratapfel baked apple, see 'Sweets, Cakes and Pastries' p. 30

Braten roast

Brathähnchen, -hendl, -huhn roast chicken, see 'National Dishes' p. 46

Bratkartoffeln see 'National Dishes' p. 46

Bratpfanne skillet, frying pan

Bratwurst see 'National Dishes' p. 46, and 'Sausages and Cold Cuts' p. 13

brauchen to need

braun brown

Brechbohnen green/string beans

brechen to break

brennen to burn

Brezel see 'Introduction' p. 6

Briefmarke postage stamp

Brieftasche wallet

Bries sweetbread

Brieswürfel see 'Regional Dishes' p. 72

Brille spectacles

bringen to bring

Broiler roast chicken, see also 'National Dishes' p. 47

Brokkoli broccoli

Brombeere blackberry

Brot bread; **Brotkorb** bread basket

Brötchen bread roll, bun, see 'Gastronomic Terms' p. 38

Brotsuppe see 'Regional Dishes' p. 62

Brotzeit see 'Gastronomic Terms' p. 38

Bruckfleisch see 'National Dishes' p. 43

Brühe stock; **Brühwürfel** stock cube

Brunsli see 'Sweets, Cakes and Pastries' p. 30

Brust breast

Bubespitzle, Buwespitz see 'National Dishes' p. 47

Buch book

Bucht bay

Buchteln see 'Sweets, Cakes and Pastries' p. 30

Buletten see 'National Dishes' p. 47

Bündner Fleisch, B. Gerstensuppe see 'National Dishes' p. 57

Bürste brush
Bus bus
Butter butter
Butterkäse see 'Cheeses' p. 17
Butterkuchen see 'Sweets, Cakes and Pastries' p. 30

Cafè see 'Where to Eat' p. 8
Camembert gebacken see 'National Dishes' p. 47
Champagner champagne
Champignon mushroom
Champignoncremesuppe see 'National Dishes' p. 47
Chateaubriand see 'National Dishes' p. 47
Chicorée chicory, endive
Cordon bleu see 'National Dishes' p. 57
Currywurst see 'Regional Dishes' p. 68

Dame lady
Dampf steam
Dampfnudel see 'Sweets, Cakes and Pastries' p. 30
danke thank you
danken to thank
dann then
dasselbe the same

Datteln dates (fruit)
Datum date
Debrecziner see 'Sausages and Cold Cuts' p. 14
Denkmal monument
desinfizieren to disinfect
Desinfektionsmittel disinfectant
Deutschland Germany; **deutsch** German
Dezember December
Diabetiker diabetic
Diät diet
dick thick
Dicke Bohnen broad bean
Dicke Bohnen mit Rauchfleisch see 'Regional Dishes' p. 71
Dienstag Tuesday
diese(r) this
Ding thing
Direktion direction
Direktor director
Diskothek disco
Dokumente documents
Donnerstag Thursday
Doppelrahm-Käse see 'Cheeses' p. 17
doppelt double
Dorsch (young) cod
Dorsch gespickt see 'Regional Dishes' p. 68

Dortmunder Export see 'Drinks' p. 21

Dose can, tin; **Dosenmilch** tinned (condensed) milk; **Dosenöffner** can opener

draußen outside

Dressing salad dressing

Duft scent, odor, aroma

dunkel dark; **Dunkles** stout (beer)

dünn thin

durch(gebraten) (meat) well done, see also 'Gastronomic Terms' p. 38

Durst thirst

Dutzend dozen

echt authentic, true

Ecke corner

Edelgulasch see 'National Dishes' p. 44

Edelpilzkäse see 'Cheeses' p. 18

egal equal

Ehefrau wife

Ehemann husband

Ei egg; **Eigelb, Eidotter** egg yolk; **Eiweiß** egg white; **hartgekochtes Ei** hard-boiled egg; **weiches Ei** soft-boiled eggs; **verlorene Eier** poached egg

Eier in Senfsoße see 'National Dishes' p. 47

Eiersalat see 'National Dishes' p. 47

Eierschwammerln chanterelle mushrooms (Austr.)

Eierspeise scrambled eggs (Austr.), egg-based dish

eigen own

Eile hurry

einfach simple

Eingang entrance

eingemacht conserved

einige some

Einkaufswagen supermarket cart

einladen invite

einschließlich included

Eintopf see 'Gastronomic Terms' p. 38

Eis ice; **Speiseeis** ice cream; **Eisdiele** ice cream parlour; **Eiswürfel** ice cube

Eisbein mit Sauerkraut see 'National Dishes' p. 47

Eiswein see 'Drinks' p. 25

Eltern parents

Emmentaler see 'Cheeses' p. 18

Ende end

Endivie endive

Endstation terminus

eng narrow, tight
englisch English, (meat) rare, see also 'Gastronomic Terms' p. 38
Ente duck
Ente mit Lübscher Füllung see 'Regional Dishes' p. 73
Entenkeulen mit Teltower Rübchen see 'Regional Dishes' p. 68
Entfernung distance
entkoffeiniert decaffeinated
Erbsen peas
Erbsensuppe see 'National Dishes' p. 47
Erdäpfel potatoes (Austr.)
Erdbeere strawberry
Erdnuß peanuts
erhalten to obtain
Erlaubnis permission
erlaubt is permitted
Errötende Jungfrau see 'Sweets, Cakes and Pastries' p. 31
Erstattung refund
erste first
Erwachsener adult
essen to eat; **Essen** food; **Essen zum Mitnehmen** takeaway food
Essig vinegar
Essigkren see 'Gastronomic Terms' p. 38

Eßkastanie chestnut
Eßlöffel tablespoon
Etikett label
etwas something
Experte expert

Faden thread
Fahrkarte ticket
Fahrplan timetable
fallen to fall
falsch wrong, false
Familie family
Farbe color
Fasan pheasant
Faschiertes ground meat (Austr.)
fast nearly, almost
Februar February
Fehler error
Feiertag public holiday
Feige fig
fein fine, delicate
Feinkostgeschäft delicatessen
Fenchel fennel
Fenster window
Ferien vacation, holidays
fertig ready
fest firm, solid
Fest party
Festbier see 'Drinks' p. 21
fett fat; **fettig** greasy

ett fat

euer fire

ilet fillet

iltern to filter

inden to find

ingernudeln see 'National Dishes' p. 48

isch fish

ischbeuschlsuppe see 'National Dishes' p. 44

ischfrikadellen see 'National Dishes' p. 48

ischpastete see 'Regional Dishes' p. 60

ischstäbchen fish fingers, fish sticks

ischsuppe fish soup

isolen green/string beans (Austr.)

lach flat

lädlsuppe see 'National Dishes' p. 44

lambiert flambé see also 'Gastronomic Terms' p. 39

lamme flame

lammeri see 'Sweets, Cakes and Pastries' p. 31

lasche bottle; **Flaschenöffner** bottle opener

leck stain

leckerlsuppe see 'National Dishes' p. 44

leisch meat

Fleischbrühe meat broth, see also 'National Dishes' p. 48

Fleischklops, Fleischkloß meatball

Fleischknödel see 'National Dishes' p. 44

Fleischpflanzerl see 'National Dishes' p. 48

Fleischwurst see 'Sausages and Cold Cuts' p. 14

Fliederbeersuppe mit Schneeklößchen see 'Regional Dishes' p. 60

Fliege fly

Flocken flakes

Flönz mit Ölk see 'Regional Dishes' p. 70

Florida see 'Gastronomic Terms' p. 38

Flug flight

Flügel wing

Flughafen airport

Flugzeug aeroplane

Flunder flounder

Fondue fondue

Fondue bourguignonne, F. neuchâteloise see 'National Dishes' p. 57

Forelle trout

Forelle blau see 'National Dishes' p. 48

Forelle mit Mandeln see 'National Dishes' p. 58

fortsetzen to continue

Foto photograph

fragen to ask; **Frage** question

Franken Franconia

Frankfurt Frankfurt

Frankfurter Kranz see 'Sweets, Cakes and Pastries' p. 31

Frankfurter Platte see 'Regional Dishes' p. 61

Frankfurter Würstchen see 'Sausages and Cold Cuts' p. 14

Fränkischer Krautbraten see 'Regional Dishes' p. 65

Frankreich France

französisch French

Frau woman, wife

frei free

Freitag Friday

Freund friend

Frikadellen meatballs, see also 'National Dishes' p. 48

Frikassee fricassee

frisch fresh

Frischling young wild boar

Frischlingskeule in der Salzkruste see 'Regional Dishes' p. 73

fritiert fried

Frittatensuppe see 'National Dishes' p. 44

Fritten French fries

Fruchtfleisch flesh, pulp (of fruit)

Frühling, Frühjahr spring

Frühlingsrolle spring rolls

Frühlingszwiebel spring onion

Frühstück breakfast

fühlen to feel

Führung guide

Füllung filling

für for

Fürst-Pückler-Eis see 'Sweets, Cakes and Pastries' p. 31

Fuß foot; **Füße** feet

Fußboden floor

Gabel fork

Gaisburger Marsch see 'Regional Dishes' p. 62

Gang (des Menüs) course

Gans goose

Gänsebraten roast goose, see also see 'National Dishes' p. 48

Gänsebrust in der Salzkruste see 'Regional Dishes' p. 61

Gänsehals, Gänseschenkel see 'Regional Dishes' p. 68, 69

Gänseleberpastete goose liver pâté

Garderobe wardrobe, coatcheck

Garnelen prawns

garnieren to garnish

Garten garden

Gärtnerinart see 'Gastronomic Terms' p. 39

Gasthaus, Gasthof, Gaststätte inn, see also 'Where to Eat' p. 9

Gebiß false teeth

Gedeck cover

Gefallen favor

gebacken baked

Gebackene Erbsen see 'Gastronomic Terms' p. 39

Gebackene Schwammerl see 'National Dishes' p. 44

geben to give

gebraten fried, roast

Geflügel poultry

gedünstet steamed

Geflügelleberwurst see 'Sausages and Cold Cuts' p. 14

gefroren frozen

gefüllt filled, stuffed

Gefüllte Paprikaschoten, Gefüllte Kalbsmedaillons see 'National Dishes' p. 49

gegen against

gegenüber opposite

gegrillt grilled, broiled

Gehacktes ground meat

gehen to go, to walk; **ausgehen** to go out (for the evening)

Geländer railing

gelb yellow; **Gelbe Rüben** carrots; **Gelbe Seiten** Yellow Pages

Geld money

Gelee aspic, jelly, jam

gemischt mixed

Gemüse vegetable

Genehmigung permission

genug enough; **genügen** to be enough

gerade (adj) straight, even, (adv) just; **geradeaus** straight ahead

geräuchert smoked

Gericht dish; court of law

gerieben grated

Germ yeast (Austr.)

Germknödel see 'Sweets, Cakes and Pastries' p. 31

Geröstel see 'Regional Dishes' p. 62

Geröstete see 'Gastronomic Terms' p. 39

Gerste barley

Gerstel see 'Gastronomic Terms' p. 39

Geruch odor

gesamt total, complete

Geschäft shop

Geschmack taste, flavor

Geschnetzeltes stew

Geschnetzeltes Kalbfleisch see 'National Dishes' p. 58

Geschoß floor, story

Gesellschaft company

gestern yesterday

getoastet toasted

Getränk drink; **alkoholisches Getränk** alcoholic drink; **alkoholfreies Getränk** soft drink

Getreide cereals

getrocknet dried

gewinnen to win

Gewürz spice; **gewürzt** spiced

Gewürzgurke pickled gherkin

Gewürznelke clove

Glas glass

glatt smooth, even

gleich same; straight away

glücklich happy

Gold gold; **goldgelb** golden

Götterspeise see 'Sweets, Cakes and Pastries' p. 31

Granatapfel pomegranate

gratis free

Graukäse see 'Cheeses' p. 18

Graupen pearl barley

Greyerzer see 'Cheeses' p. 18

Grieß semolina

Grießnockerlnsuppe see 'National Dishes' p. 44

Grill grill; **vom Grill** grilled

Gri Soos see *Rinderburst*, 'Regional Dishes' p. 62

grob coarse, rough

Gröner Heinrich see 'Regional Dishes' p. 74

groß big, tall

Größe size

Grumbeerküchle see 'National Dishes' p. 49

grün green, see also 'Gastronomic Terms' p. 39

grüne Bohnen green beans

Grüner Aal see 'Regional Dishes' p. 60

Grüne Soße see 'Gastronomic Terms' p. 39

Grünkohl kale

Grünkohl mit Kasseler und Pinkel see 'Regional Dishes' p. 74

Gruppe group; **Gruppenleiter** group leader

G'selchtes see 'Regional Dishes' p. 66

G'spritzter see 'Drinks' p. 26

Guglhupf see 'Sweets, Cakes and Pastries' p. 32

Gulasch, Gulaschsuppe see 'National Dishes' p. 44

Gurke cucumber

gut good, well

Guten Appetit! Bon Apétit!

haben to have

hacken to chop

Hackfleisch ground meat

Hafer oats; Haferflocken oatflakes

Haferl large cup

Hagebuttentee rosehip tea

Hähnchen (roast) chicken

Hähnchenkeulen in körniger Senfsauce see 'Regional Dishes' p. 72

halb, Hälfte half

Halbfett-Käse half-fat cheese

Halle hall, room

halten to hold, to keep

Haltestelle stop

Halve Hahn see 'Regional Dishes' p. 71

Hamburger Fischsuppe see 'Regional Dishes' p. 60

Hammel mutton

Hammelbraten roast mutton

Hammelfleisch mutton

Hammelkoteletts auf grünen Bohnen see 'National Dishes' p. 49

Hand hand

Handbuch manual

Handkäse see 'Cheeses' p. 18 and 'Regional Dishes' p. 62

Handschuhe gloves

Handtasche handbag, purse

Handtuch towel

hart hard

Hartkäse see 'Cheeses' p. 17

Harzer see 'Cheeses' p. 18

Hase hare

Haselnüsse hazelnuts

Hasenbraten roast hare

Hasenpfeffer see 'National Dishes' p. 49

Hasenterrine, Hasenkuchen see 'Regional Dishes' p. 63

häßlich ugly

Hauptgericht main course

Häuptlsalat lettuce (Austr.)

hauptsächlich principal, principally

Haus house im Haus at home

Hausfrauenart see 'Gastronomic Terms' p. 39

hausgemacht homemade

Hausmacherart see 'Gastronomic Terms' p. 39

Hausmannskost homestyle cooking

Hauswein house wine

Hawaii see 'Gastronomic Terms' p. 39

Haxe shank

Hecht pike

Hechtenkraut see 'Regional Dishes' p. 66

Hefe yeast; **Hefeteig** leavened pastry/dough

Hefeweizen see 'Drinks' p. 23

Heidelammkeule see 'Regional Dishes' p. 64

Heilbutt halibut

heiß hot

heizen to heat

Heizung heating

helfen to help

Helles lager

Hering herring

Heringssalat see 'National Dishes' p. 49 and 'Recipes' p. 76

Herr Mr

Heuriger see 'Where to Eat' p. 9

heute today; **heute abend** this evening

hier here

Hilfe help

Himbeere raspberry

Himmel sky, heaven

Himmel und Erde see 'Regional Dishes' p. 71 and 'Recipes' p. 77

hinter behind

hinterlegen to deposit

Hinweise directions, instructions; **hinweisen** to indicate

Hirn brain

Hirnsuppe see 'Regional Dishes' p. 63

Hirsch deer, venison

hoch high

Hochstuhl highchair

Hochzeit wedding

Holland Holland; **holländisch** Dutch

Holländische Soße see 'Gastronomic Terms' p. 40

Holz wood

Honig honey; **Honigmelone** honeydew melon

hören to hear

Hotel hotel

Huhn chicken

Hühnerfrikassee see 'National Dishes' p. 49 and 'Recipes' p. 78

Hülsenfrüchte pulses

Hummer lobster

hundert hundred

Hunger hunger

Hut hat

Imbiß snack

Imbiß(stube) snack bar, see 'Where to Eat' p. 9

immer always

Information information; **informieren** to inform

Ingwer ginger

Innereien offal

Insekt insect

Irrtum error

Italien Italy

ja yes

Jacke(tt) jacket

Jägerart see 'Gastronomic Terms' p. 40

Jägerschnitzel see 'National Dishes' p. 49

Jahr year; **Jahrgang** vintage

Jahreszeit season

Januar January

jeder each

jemand someone

jetzt now

Joghurt yoghurt

Johannisbeere schwarze blackcurrants; **J. rote** redcurrants

Jugendherberge youth hostel

Juli July

jung young

Junge boy

Jungfernbraten see 'National Dishes' p. 44

Juni June

Kabeljau cod

Kabeljau in Senfsauce see 'Regional Dishes' p. 69

Kabeljau nach Hamburger Art see 'Regional Dishes' p. 60

Kaffee coffee, see also 'Drinks' p. 27; **Kaffee mit Milch** coffee with a drop of milk; **koffeinfreier Kaffee** decaffeinated coffee

Kaffeehaus see 'Where to Eat' p. 9

Kaiserfleisch see 'National Dishes' p. 44

Kaiserschmarrn see 'Sweets, Cakes and Pastries' p. 31

Kaiserschnitzel see 'National Dishes' p. 49

Kakao cocoa
Kalb vealcalf
Kalbfleisch veal
Kalbsbraten roast veal
Kalbsfrikasse see 'National Dishes' p. 49
Kalbshaxe see 'Regional Dishes' p. 66
Kalbsleber Berliner Art see 'Regional Dishes' p. 68
Kalbsnieren in Senfsoße see 'Regional Dishes' p. 71
Kalbssteak Cordon Bleu see 'Recipes' p. 79
Kalorien calories
kalt cold
Kaltschale see 'Gastronomic Terms' p. 40
Kamille camomile
kandiert candied
Kandiszucker candy
Kaninchen rabbit
Kännchen jug
Kapaun capon
Kapern capers
kaputt broken
Karaffe caraffe, jug
Karamel caramel; **Karamelpudding** crème caramel
Karfiol cauliflower; **auf Wiener Art** see 'National Dishes' p. 45

Karpfen carp
Karpfen mit Buttersauce see 'Regional Dishes' p. 68
Karte map
Kartoffel potato
Kartoffelgratin, -klöße, -plätzchen, -puffer, see 'National Dishes' p. 50 and 'Recipes' p. 81
Kartoffelpüree, -salat, -suppe see 'National Dishes' p. 50, 51 and 'Recipes' p. 81
Kartoffelscheiben (überbacken) see 'Regional Dishes' p. 72
Kartoffelstrudel see 'Regional Dishes' p. 66
Käse cheese
Käsefondue, Käseschnitte Oberländer Art, Käsewähe see 'National Dishes' p. 58
Käsekuchen, Käsesahnetorte see 'Sweets, Cakes and Pastries' p. 32
Kasse till
Kasseler smoked pork chop in brine
Kasseler mit Sauerkraut see 'National Dishes' p. 51
Katenwurst see 'Sausages and Cold Cuts' p. 14

kauen to chew

kaufen to buy

Kaviar caviar, see also 'Regional Dishes' p. 70

Kehle throat

keiner no-one

Kekse biscuits

Keller cellar

Kellner waiter; **Kellnerin** waitress

Kerze candle

Keule (eg chicken) leg

Kichererbsen chickpeas

Kieler Sprotten see 'Regional Dishes' p. 74

Kind baby, child

kinderfreundlich ideal for children

Kinderwagen baby carriage, pram

Kipfel, Kipferl see 'Sweets, Cakes and Pastries' p. 32

Kirchweih festival

Kirsche cherry

Kirschstreusel see 'Sweets, Cakes and Pastries' p. 32

Kissen cushion

Kiwi kiwi fruit

klar clear, transparent; **Klarer** see 'Drinks' p. 27

Kleie bran

klein little

Klimaanlage air conditioning

Kloß dumpling, meatball

Knäckebrot rye cracker

knackig crunchy

Kneipe pub, see 'Where to Eat' p. 11

Knoblauch garlic

Knochen bone

Knödel dumplings, see 'Gastronomic Terms' p. 40 and 'Recipes' p. 80

Knopf button

Knöpfle see 'Regional Dishes' p. 63

knusprig crunchy

Koch cook (male); **Köchin** cook (female)

kochen to cook, to boil; **kochend** boiling

Kochfleisch boiled meat

Kochkäse see 'Cheeses' p. 18

Kochsalat see 'National Dishes' p. 45

Kochschinken ham

koffeinfrei decaffeinated

Koffer suitcase

Kohl cabbage

Kohlrouladen see 'National Dishes' p. 51 and 'Recipes' p. 82

Kohlsprossen Brussels sprouts (Austr.)

Kokosnuß coconut

Kolatschen see 'Sweets, Cakes and Pastries' p. 32

Köln Cologne

Kölsch see 'Drinks' p. 21

kommen to come

Konditorei cakeshop, see 'Where to Eat' p. 10

Königinpastete see 'National Dishes' p. 51

Königsberger Klopse see 'National Dishes' p. 51

Königskuchen see 'Sweets, Cakes and Pastries' p. 32

können to be able to, can

Konservierungsstoffe preservatives

Kontaktlinsen contact lenses

kontrollieren to check

Kopf head; **Kopfschmerzen** headache

Kopfsalat lettuce

Korn corn, see also 'Drinks' p. 27

Kosten cost; **kosten** to cost

Kotelett cutlet, chop

Krabben prawns

Krabbensalat, -cocktail see 'National Dishes' p. 51

Krach noise

Krakauer see 'Sausages and Cold Cuts' p. 14

krank ill

Krankenhaus hospital

Krapfen donut, see 'Sweets, Cakes and Pastries' p. 30

Kratzete see 'Regional Dishes' p. 63

Kräuter herbs

Krautsalat, Krautwickel see 'National Dishes' p. 51 and 'Recipes' p. 82

Krawatte tie

Krebs crab

Kreditkarte credit card

Kren horseradish (Austr.)

Krenfleisch see 'National Dishes' p. 45

Kresse watercress

Krokette croquette

Küche kitchen, cooking, cuisine

Kuchen cake, tart

Kühlschrank refrigerator

Kukuruz maize (Austr.)

Kümmel cumin

Kunde client

Kürbis pumpkin

kurz short

Küste coast

Kutteln tripe

Labskaus see 'Regional Dishes' p. 61

Lachs salmon

Laib bread roll

Lakritz liquorice

Lamm lamb; **Lammbraten** roast lamb

Lammhaxen auf Bohnenpüree see 'Regional Dishes' p. 65

Land country, land (region in Germany); **auf dem Land** in the countryside

Landjäger see 'Sausages and Cold Cuts' p. 14

lang long

langsam slow

Languste lobster

lassen to leave

Laubfrösche (lit. tree frog!), see 'Regional Dishes' p. 63

Lauch leek

laut loud

Lebensmittelfarbstoffe food coloring

Lebensmittelvergiftung food poisoning

Leber liver

Leber- und Nierenpfanne see 'Regional Dishes' p. 66

Leberkäs see 'Regional Dishes' p. 66

Leberknödel, Leberknödelsuppe see 'Regional Dishes' p. 66 and 'Recipes' p. 83

Leberwurst see 'Sausages and Cold Cuts' p. 14

Lebkuchen, Lebkucheneis see 'Sweets, Cakes and Pastries' p. 33

Leckerli see 'Sweets, Cakes and Pastries' p. 33

leer empty

leicht light

Leipziger Allerlei see 'Regional Dishes' p. 73

Leitung direction (*cinema*), (electric) cable

Lende loin; **Lendenbraten** roast loin

Lese harvest

lesen to read

letzte last

Licht light

lieb nice, dear

Liebesknochen see 'Sweets, Cakes and Pastries' p. 33

Lied song

Likör liquer

Limburger see 'Cheeses' p. 18

Limonade lemonade

Linsen lentils

Linsen auf Schwäbische Art see 'Regional Dishes' p. 63

LIN-MÄR

Linsensuppe see 'National Dishes' p. 51

Linzer Torte see 'Sweets, Cakes and Pastries' p. 33

Liste list

Liter liter

Löffel spoon

lohnend convenient

Lokal pub, bar, see also 'Where to Eat' p. 11

Lorbeerblatt bay leaf

löslich soluble; **löslicher Kaffee** instant coffee

Lübeck Lubecke

Lübecker Matrosenfleisch see 'Regional Dishes' p. 74

Luft air

Lunge lung

Lungenbraten see 'National Dishes' p. 45

Lüngerl see 'Regional Dishes' p. 66

Lutscher lollipop

Lyoner Wurst see 'Sausages and Cold Cuts' p. 14

machen to make, to have

Mädchen girl

Magen stomach

Magenbitter bitters, (after-dinner) liquer

Magenschmerzen stomach ache

mager thin, lean

Mager-Käse low-fat cheese

Mahlzeit meal; **(gesegnete) M.!** Bon appétit! Enjoy your meal!

Mai May

Mais corn, maize; **Maiskolben** corn on the cob

Majoran marjoram

Makrele clear, empty

makrobiotisch macrobiotic

Malzbier see 'Drinks' p. 22

Mandarine mandarine

Mandeln almonds

Mangold chard

Mann man

Marillen apricot (Austr.)

Marillenknödel see 'Sweets, Cakes and Pastries' p. 33

Marinade marinade

Markklößchensuppe see 'Regional Dishes' p. 66

Markt market

Marmelade marmalade

Marmorkuchen see 'Sweets, Cakes and Pastries' p. 33

Maronen chestnuts, see also 'Regional Dishes' p. 73

März March

Märzenbier see 'Drinks' p. 22

Marzipan marzipan

Maßkrug beer glass holding one liter

Matjesfilet marinated herring fillets, see also 'Regional Dishes' p. 61

Maultaschen see 'Regional Dishes' p. 63

Mayonnaise mayonnaise

Mecklenburg Mecklenberg

Mecklenburger Rippenbraten see 'Regional Dishes' p. 69

Medaillons medallions, see also 'Gastronomic Terms' p. 40

medium (meat) medium, see 'Gastronomic Terms' p. 40

Medizin medicine

Meer sea

Meeresfrüchte seafood

Meerrettich horseradish

Mehl flour

Mehlspeise see 'Gastronomic Terms' p. 40

mehr more

Mehrwertsteuer VAT

Melange see 'Drinks' p. 27

Melone melon

Messer knife

Mett see 'Gastronomic Terms' p. 40

Mettwurst see 'Sausages and Cold Cuts' p. 15

Metzelsuppe see 'Regional Dishes' p. 63

Metzger butcher

Miesmuscheln mussles, see *Muscheln*

mieten to hire, to rent

Mikrowelle microwave oven

Milch milk; **Milchkaffee** white coffee; **Milchpulver** powdered milk

Milchbrötchen milk bread

Milchprodukte dairy products

Milchrahmstrudel, Millirahmstrudel see 'Sweets, Cakes and Pastries' p. 33

Milz spleen

Milzwurst see 'Sausages and Cold Cuts' p. 15

Mineralwasser mineral water

Minute minute

Minze mint

Mischung mixture

Mißverständnis misunderstood

mit with

Mittag midday

Mittagessen lunch

Mitte middle, half
Mittel means, remedy
Mittwoch Wednesday
mögen to like
möglich possible
Mohn poppy seeds;
   Mohnstriezel see 'Sweets,
   Cakes and Pastries' p. 33
Möhre, Mohrrübe carrot
**Mohrenkopf, Mohr im
   Hemd** see 'Sweets, Cakes
   and Pastries' p. 34
Monat month
Montag Monday
Morgen morning; **morgen**
   tomorrow
Mosel Moselle
Most must, cider
Mozartkugeln see 'Sweets,
   Cakes and Pastries' p. 34
Mücke mosquito
Müll garbage
Müllerinart see
   'Gastronomic Terms' p. 40
München Munich
Münchner from Munich, see
   also 'Drinks' p. 22
Mund mouth
Münze coin
Mürbeteig shortcrust pastry
Muscheln mussels

Muscheln in Weißweinsud
   see 'Regional Dishes' p. 71
Muschelschale shell
Museum museum
Musik music
Muskatnuß nutmeg
Müsli v. *Bircher Müsli*,
   'National Dishes' p. 57
müssen must, to have to
Mutter mother

nach after, towards
nachher afterwards
Nachname surname
Nachricht message
Nachspeise dessert
Nacht night
Nachtisch dessert
Nacken nape of the neck
nah near
Name name
Napfkuchen see 'Sweets,
   Cakes and Pastries' p. 34
naß wet
Natur nature, natural
natürlich naturally, certainly
neben next to
nehmen to take
Nektarine nectarine
Nelke clove
nett nice, kind

eu new
Neujahr New Year
nicht not; **nichts** nothing
Nichtraucher non-smoking
nie never
niedrig low
niemand no-one
Nieren kidneys
noch still, yet
Nockerln see 'Gastronomic
  Terms' p. 40
Norden north
Nougat nougat
November November
Nudeln noodles
Nummer number
nur only
Nürnberg Nuremberg
Nürnberger Rostbratwurst
  see 'Sausages and Cold
  Cuts' p. 15
Nuß nut; **Nußknacker**
  nutcracker;
  Nußschokolade hazelnut
  chocolate

Obazda see 'Regional
  Dishes' p. 67
Oberpfälzer Krengemüse see
  'Regional Dishes' p. 69
Obers cream (Austr.)
Obst fruit; **Obstsaft** fruit
  juice; **Obstsalat** fruit salad;

Obstkuchen fruit tart
Ochse ox
**Ochsenbrust mit
  Meerrettich,
  Ochsenschwanzsuppe** see
  'National Dishes' p. 51
Ochsenmaulsalat see
  'Regional Dishes' p. 67
Ochsenschwanzragout see
  'Regional Dishes' p. 62
Ofen oven
Ofenkartoffel see
  'Gastronomic Terms' p. 41
Ofenschlupfer see 'Sweets,
  Cakes and Pastries' p. 34
oft often
ohne without
ohnmächtig fainted
Ohrring earring
Oktober October;
  Oktoberfest see 'Where to
  Eat' p. 12
Öl oil; **ölig** oily, greasy
Oliven olives
Omelett omelet
Orangensaft orange juice
Oregano oregano
originell original
Ort place
Ostern Easter
Österreich Austria;
  Österreicher Austrian

Paar a pair; **ein paar** some
Päckchen packet
Palatschinken see 'Sweets, Cakes and Pastries' p. 34
Pampelmuse grapefruit
panieren to coat with breadcrumbs
Paniermehl breadcrumbs
Papiertaschentuch paper tissue
Paprika bell pepper
Paprika-Huhn see 'National Dishes' p. 45
Paprikaschnitzel see 'National Dishes' p. 52
Paradeiser tomatoes (Austr.)
Park park
Parkplatz carpark
Paß passport
passieren to happen
Pellkartoffeln potatoes boiled in their skins
Perlhuhn guinea fowl
Personalausweis identity card
Petersilie parsley
Petersilienkartoffeln see 'Gastronomic Terms' p. 41
Pfanne skillet, frying pan
Pfannengerichte see 'Gastronomic Terms' p. 41
Pfannfisch see 'Regional Dishes' p. 74

Pfannkuchen see 'Gastronomic Terms' p. 4
Pfeffer pepper; **Pfeffermühl** peppermill
Pfefferkuchen peppered bread
Pfefferminztee peppermint tea
Pfefferpotthast see 'Regiona Dishes' p. 71
Pfirsich peach
Pfirsich Melba see 'Sweets, Cakes and Pastries' p. 34
Pflaster sticking plaster
Pflaume plum
Pflaumenkuchen see 'Sweets, Cakes and Pastries' p. 34
Pflicht duty
Pichelsteiner Topf see 'Regional Dishes' p. 67 and 'Recipes' p. 84
Pille pill
Pillekuchen see 'Regional Dishes' p. 71
Pils, Pilsener, Pilsner see 'Drinks' p. 23
Pilze mushrooms
Pinte pub, see also 'Where to Eat' p. 11
Pistazien pistacchios
Plan plan, map

latz square, seat

lockwurst see 'Sausages and Cold Cuts' p. 15

ökelfleisch meat in brine

ommesbude see *Imbiß* p. 9

ommes frites French fries

ortion portion

ostkarte postcard

oularde young chicken for fattening

owidl plum sauce (Austr.)

ralinen chocolate, praline

reis price

reiselbeere cranberry

reßsack see 'Sausages and Cold Cuts' p. 15

rinten see 'Sweets, Cakes and Pastries' p. 34

rinzregententorte see 'Sweets, Cakes and Pastries' p. 34

robieren to taste, to try

rost! Prosit! Cheers!

udding pudding

uder powder, talcum powder; **Puderzucker** confectioner's sugar, icing sugar

ulver dust

ute turkey

uter turkey

uterbraten roast turkey

Puter in Aspik see 'Sausages and Cold Cuts' p. 15

Qualität quality

Quark, quark, cottage cheese, see also 'Cheeses' p. 18

Quarknudeln see 'National Dishes' p. 52

Quitte quince

Quittung receipt

Raclette see 'Cheeses' p. 18 and 'National Dishes' p. 58

Radi radish, see also 'National Dishes' p. 45

Radieschen radish

Radieschenquark mit Kümmelkartoffeln see 'Regional Dishes' p. 69

Radio radio

Radler see 'Drinks' p. 26

Ragout fin see 'National Dishes' p. 52

Rahm cream, custard (Austr.)

Rahmsulz see 'Sweets, Cakes and Pastries' p. 35

Ranzenstecher see 'National Dishes' p. 52

Ratsherrentopf see 'National Dishes' p. 58

Ratskeller see 'Where to Eat' p. 10

Rauchbier see 'Drinks' p. 23

rauchen to smoke

Raucher smoker

Räucherhering smoked herring

Räucherlachs smoked salmon

Räucherschinken smoked ham

Räucherspeck smoked lard

Rauchfleisch, Räucherfleisch smoked meat

Raumtemperatur room temperature

Rebhuhn partridge

Rebhuhn im Weinblatt see 'Regional Dishes' p. 70

Rechnung bill, invoice

rechte (r) right; **rechts** to the right

Regenmantel raincoat

Regensburger see 'Sausages and Cold Cuts' p. 15

Regenschirm umbrella

Region region

Reh roebuck

Rehrücken see 'Regional Dishes' p. 63, 64 and 'Sweets, Cakes and Pastries' p. 35

Reibekuchen, Reiberdatschi see 'National Dishes' p. 52

reif mature, ripe

Reis rice

Reiseführer guide

Reis Trauttmansdorff see 'Sweets, Cakes and Pastries' p. 35

reservieren to book; **reserviert** reserved; **Reservierung** reservation

Rest rest, leftovers

Restaurant restaurant, see 'Where to Eat' p. 10

Rezept receipt, prescription

Rhabarber rhubarb

Rhabarber-Kompott see 'Sweets, Cakes and Pastries' p. 35

Rhein Rhine; **Rheinland** Rhineland

Ribisel currant (Austr.)

richtig right

Richtung direction

riechen to smell

Rieslinghuhn see 'Regional Dishes' p. 70

Rind beef; **Rinderbraten** roast beef

Rinderbrust mit Grüner Soße see 'Regional Dishes' p. 62

Rinderrouladen see 'National Dishes' p. 52 and 'Recipes' p. 85

Rinderzunge see 'National Dishes' p. 52

Rindfleisch beef

Rindfleisch mit Pflaumen see 'Regional Dishes' p. 69

Rippchen spare ribs; cutlet

Rogen fish roe

Roggen rye; **Roggenbrot** ryebread

roh raw; **roher Schinken** cured ham

Rohrnudel see 'Sweets, Cakes and Pastries' p. 35

Rohrzucker cane sugar

Rollmops mit Kartoffelsalat see 'National Dishes' p. 52

Romadur see 'Cheeses' p. 19

Röntgenbild X-ray

Rosenkohl Brussels sprouts

Rosinen raisin

Rosmarin rosemary

Rost grill; **vom Rost** grilled, broiled

Rostbraten grilled meat

Rostbraten Esterhazy see 'National Dishes' p. 45

Rostbratwurst see 'Sausages and Cold Cuts' p. 15

rösten to grill, to roast

Rösti see 'National Dishes' p. 58

rot red

Rote Bete beetroot

Rote-Bete-Salat see 'National Dishes' p. 52

Rote Grütze see 'Sweets, Cakes and Pastries' p. 35 and 'Recipes' p. 85

Rote Rübe beetroot

Rotkohl red cabbage, and see 'National Dishes' p. 53

Rotwein red wine

Rouladen roulade

Rübe turnip

Rübenkraut see 'Gastronomic Terms' p. 41

Rückkehr return

rückwärts backwards

ruhig calm, tranquil

Rührei scrambled eggs

Rum rum

Rumpsteak rump steak, see 'National Dishes' p. 53

Rumtopf see 'Sweets, Cakes and Pastries' p. 35

rund round

Russe see 'Drinks' p. 26

Saccharin saccharine

Sachertorte see 'Sweets, Cakes and Pastries' p. 35 and 'Recipes' p. 86

Safran saffron

Saft juice; **frisch ausgepreßt** freshly squeezed juice

sagen to say

Sahne cream, custard

Sahnehering see 'National Dishes' p. 53

Salami salami

Salat salad; **Salatsoße** salad dressing

Salbei sage

Salm salmon

Salm nach Basler Art see 'National Dishes' p. 58

Salz salt; **salzig** salty; **gesalzen** with salt; **Salzstreuer** salt cellar

Salzburg Salzburg

Salzburger Nockerln see 'Sweets, Cakes and Pastries' p. 36 and 'Recipes' p. 87

Salzhering salted herring

Salzkartoffeln boiled potatoes

Samen seed

Samstag Saturday

Sardelle anchovy; **Sardellenpaste** anchovy paste

Sardinen sardines

Sau sow (female pig); **Saubohnen** broad beans

Saumagen see 'Regional Dishes' p. 70

sauber clean; **saubermachen** to clean

sauer sour, see 'Gastronomic Terms' p. 41; **saure Sahne** soured cream

Sauerampfer sorrel

Sauerampfersuppe see 'National Dishes' p. 53

Sauerbraten, Sauerkraut see 'National Dishes' p. 53 and 'Recipes' p. 88, 90

Sauermilch-Käse see 'Cheeses' p. 17

Sauerrahm soured cream

Saure Klopse, Saure Kutteln see 'National Dishes' p. 54

Sbrinz see 'Cheeses' p. 19

Schabziger see 'Cheeses' p. 19

Schale bowl; **schälen** to peel

Schanigarten see 'Where to Eat' p. 10

scharf spicy

Schaschlik(spieß) see 'National Dishes' p. 54

Scheck check (cheque)

Scheibe slice

Scheiterhaufen see 'Sweets, Cakes and Pastries' p. 36

Schellfisch haddock

Schichtkäse see 'Cheeses' p. 19

Schinken ham; **gekochter Sch.** cooked ham; **roher Sch.** cured ham

Schinken im Brotteig see 'National Dishes' p. 54

Schinkennudeln see 'National Dishes' p. 54

Schinkenspeck, Schinkenwurst see 'Sausages and Cold Cuts' p. 15

Schlachtplatte see 'National Dishes' p. 54

schlagen to beat, to hit

Schlagobers whipped cream (Austr.)

Schlagsahne whipped cream (Ger.)

Schlange snake

schlecht bad

Schlesische Häckerle see 'National Dishes' p. 54

schließen to close; **geschlossen** closed

schmackhaft tasty

Schmalz lard

Schmelz-Käse soft cheese

Schmerz pain

schmoren to braise, to cook over a slow heat; **Schmorbraten** braised

schmutzig dirty

Schnaps see 'Drinks' p. 27

Schnecke snail, see also 'Sweets, Cakes and Pastries' p. 36

Schneckensuppe see 'Regional Dishes' p. 64

schneiden to cut

schnell fast

Schnibbelbohnen mit Gehacktem see 'Regional Dishes' p. 71

Schnibbelkuchen see 'Regional Dishes' p. 71

Schnitte slice, see 'Gastronomic Terms' p. 41

Schnitt-Käse cheese (hard cheese for slicing)

Schnittlauch chives

Schnitzel cutlet

Schnitzel Holstein see 'National Dishes' p. 54

Schnuller dummy, pacifier, comforter

Schokolade chocolate; **heiße Schokolade** hot chocolate

Scholle plaice

Schollenfilets auf Finkenwerder Art see 'Regional Dishes' p. 61

schön beautiful
Schöpsernes mutton (Austr.)
schreiben to write
Schulter shoulder
Schupfnudeln see 'National Dishes' p. 55
schütten to pour
Schützenfest shooting party
schwach weak
Schwämme, Schwammerln mushrooms (Austr.)
schwanger pregnant
schwarz black
Schwarzbrot wholemeal bread
Schwarzwald Black Forest
Schwarzwälder Kirschtorte see 'Sweets, Cakes and Pastries' p. 36
Schwarzwurzelgemüse see 'Regional Dishes' p. 73
Schwein pig
Schweinebauch bacon
Schweinebraten roast pig
Schweinefleisch pork
Schweinshaxe see 'Regional Dishes' p. 67 and 'Recipes' p. 91
Schweinskopfsülze see 'Sausages and Cold Cuts' p. 15
Schweinsohren see 'Sweets, Cakes and Pastries' p. 36

Schweiz Switzerland; **schweizerisch** Swiss
schwer heavy
Schwertfisch swordfish
schwierig difficult
Schwimmbad swimming poo
schwimmen to go swimming
Schwyzer Käsesuppe see 'National Dishes' p. 59
See lake
Seezunge sole
Seezunge Müllerinart see 'National Dishes' p. 55
sehen to see
sehr much
Seife soap
Seite side
Sekt sparkling wine
Selchfleisch smoked meat (Austr.)
Sellerie celery
Selleriesalat see 'National Dishes' p. 55
Semmel bread roll, see 'Gastronomic Terms' p. 38; **Semmelbrösel** breadcrumbs
Semmelknödel see 'Regiona Dishes' p. 67
Senf mustard, see also 'Gastronomic Terms' p. 4
September September

Serviette napkin
Sicherheitsnadel safety pin
Sirup syrup
Sitz(platz) seat, place (to sit)
sofort immediately
Sohn son
Soja soya
Sojabohnensprossen beansprouts
Sojasoße soy sauce
Sommer summer; **sommerlich** summer (adj)
Sonntag Sunday
Soße sauce
Spanferkel roast suckling pig
Spargel asparagus
Spargel mit Holländischer Soße, Spargelcremesuppe, Spargelröllchen see 'National Dishes' p. 55
Spätlese see 'Drinks' p. 25
Spätzle see 'Regional Dishes' p. 64
spazierengehen to walk, to go for a walk
Speck smoked bacon, pork fat
Speckkuchen see 'Regional Dishes' p. 64
Speisekarte menu
Spezi see 'Drinks' p. 26
Spezialität speciality, see also 'Gastronomic Terms' p. 41

Spiegelei fried egg
Spiel game; **spielen** to play
Spieß spit, (skewer)
Spinat spinach
Spital hospital (Austr.)
Sprossen shoots, buds
sprudelnd fizzy; **Sprudelwasser** sparkling mineral water
Stäbchen (fish) fingers
Stachelbeere gooseberry
Stadt city
Stärke (Kraft) strength; **Speisestärke** starch
statt instead of
Steak steak, see also 'Gastronomic Terms' p. 41
Steinpilze porcini mushrooms
Stielmus in Sahnesauce see 'Regional Dishes' p. 71
stilles Wasser still mineral water
Stockwerk floor, story
Stöpsel cork, stopper
stören to disturb
Strammer Max see 'National Dishes' p. 55
Straße street, road
Strauß bunch, bouquet; ostrich
Streichhölzer matches

Streuselkuchen see 'Sweets, Cakes and Pastries' p. 36

Strom (electric) current

Strudel see 'Sweets, Cakes and Pastries' p. 36

Stube, Stüberl pub, see 'Where to Eat' p. 11

Stück piece, slice

Stuhl chair

Stunde hour

Sturm storm

Süden south

Sülze gelatine, aspic

Sülzkotelett, Sülzwurst see 'Sausages and Cold Cuts' p. 15, 16

Suppe soup

Suppentopf soup tureen, see also 'Gastronomic Terms' p. 42

süß sweet

Süßigkeiten, Süßwaren sweets, confectionery

süßsauer sweet-and-sour

Süßstoff sweetener

Tabakwarenladen tabacconist`s

Tablett tray

Tablette tablet

Tafelspitz see 'National Dishes' p. 45

Tag day

Tageskarte menu of the day

Tagessuppe soup of the day

Tageszeitung daily

tanzen to dance

Tatar see 'Gastronomic Terms' p. 42

Tasche pocket, purse, handbag

Taschentuch handkerchief

Tasse cup

Taube pigeon

tausend thousand

Tee tea

Teebeutel teabag

Teelöffel teaspoon

Teewurst smoked sausage paste, see 'Sausages and Cold Cuts' p. 16

Teig dough, pastry

Teil part

Telefon telephone

Telefonanruf telephone call

Telefonbuch telephone directory

Teller plate, dish; **Tellerfleisch** see 'National Dishes' p. 45

Temperatur temperature

Tempo(taschentuch) paper tissue

Terrasse terrace

Terrine terrine, soup tureen

teuer expensive
Thunfisch tuna;
    Thunfischsalat tuna salad
Thymian thyme
tief deep
Tilsiter see 'Cheeses' p. 19
Tintenfisch squid
Tirol Tyrol
**Tiroler Gröstl, Tiroler
    Knödel** see 'National
    Dishes' p. 45
Tisch table
Tischdecke tablecloth
toasten toast
Tochter daughter
Toilette restrooms;
    Toilettenpapier toilet
    paper
Tomate tomato
Tomatencremesuppe see
    'National Dishes' p. 55
Topf saucepan
Topfen cottage cheese
    (Austr.)
tragen to carry, to wear
Trauben grape
treffen to meet
Treppe staircase
trinken to drink
Trinkgeld to tip
Trinkwasser drinking water

trocken dry
Trockenobst dried fruit
Trockenpflaume prune
Trüffel truffle
Truthahn turkey
tun to do
Tunke sauce
Tür door

überbacken to cook au
    gratin
überfüllt overcrowded
übrigbleiben to remain
Uhr clock
umdrehen to turn
Umgebung surroundings
Umschlag envelope
unangenehm unpleasant
unbequem uncomfortable
unmöglich impossible
unten under
unter under; **unterhalb**
    underneath
Unterschrift signature

vakuumverpackt vaccuum-
    packed
Vanille vanilla
**Vanilleeis mit heißen
    Himbeeren** see 'Sweets,
    Cakes and Pastries' p. 36
Vanillekipferl see 'Sweets,
    Cakes and Pastries' p. 36

VEG-WÄH

Vegetarier vegetarian
Verabredung appointment
verbindlich binding
verbrannt burnt
verdaulich digestible
Verdauungsbeschwerden indigestion
verdorben ruined, spoilt
Verfallsdatum 'Best Before' date
vergessen to forget
Vergnügen fun, entertainment
verkaufen to sell
verlassen to leave, to abandon
verlieren to lose; **verloren** lost
verlobt fiancé(e)
verlorene Eier poached eggs
vermeiden to avoid
Versagen failure
verschieden different
Verschleiertes Bauernmädchen see 'Sweets, Cakes and Pastries' p. 36
Verspätung delay, lateness
Verstand reason, mind
verstehen to understand
versuchen to try, to attempt
vertraut familiar
viel much, many

vielleicht perhaps
Vierländer Poularde see 'Regional Dishes' p. 61
Viertel quarter
Vitamine vitamins
voll full; **vollmundig** full-bodied
Vollfett-Käse full-fat cheese
Vollkorn- wholewheat
Vollkornbrot wholewheat bread
Vollkornreis brown rice
Vollmilch full-fat milk; **Vollmilchschokolade** milk chocolate
vollständig full
vorn in front of
vorsichtig sensible
Vorspeise appetizer, starter
Vorstellung show
vorwärts forward
vorziehen to prefer

Wacholder juniper
wachsam careful
Wachtel quail
Waffel wafer, see 'Sweets, Cakes and Pastries' p. 37
Waffeltüte (ice cream) cone
während while, during
Währung currency

Waldfrüchte wild berries

Walnüsse walnuts

Wand wall

wann when

warm warm; **wärmen** to warm up

warnen to warn

warten to wait

warum? why?

was? what?

waschen to wash

Wasser water

wasserdicht waterproof, watertight

Wasserhahn fawcett, tap

Wassermelone watermelon

wechseln to change; **Wechsel** change, promissary note; **Wechselkurs** exchange rate

Weg path, way

weg way

wegnehmen to remove

weich soft

Weihnachten Christmas

weil because

Wein wine; **Weinhandlung** wineseller; **Weinkarte** wine list

Weinbergschnecke snail

Weinkeller, Weinstube see 'Where to Eat' p. 10

Weinprobe wine tasting

Weinschorle see 'Drinks' p. 26

Weinsuppe see 'Regional Dishes' p. 70

weiß white

Weißbier see 'Drinks' p. 23

Weißbrot white bread

Weißkäse see 'Cheeses' p. 19

Weißwein white wine

Weißwürste see 'Regional Dishes' p. 67 and 'Sausages and Cold Cuts' p. 16

weit far

Weizen grain

Weizenbier, Weizenbock, Weizendunkel see 'Drinks' p. 23

welcher? which?

wenig little; **ein wenig** a little; **weniger** less

wenigstens at least

wenn if, when

wer? who?

werfen to throw

Wespe wasp

wichtig important

wie how; **wieviel?** how much?; **wie viele?** how many?

Wien Vienna
Wiener Schnitzel see 'National Dishes' p. 45
Wiener Würstchen see 'Sausages and Cold Cuts' p. 16
wild wild
Wild(bret) game (meat)
Wildente (gebraten) mit Zitronensauce see 'Regional Dishes' p. 69
Wildleder suede
Wildschwein wild boar
willkommen welcome
Wind wind
Windbeutel cream puff
Windel nappy, diaper
Winter winter
wirklich really
wissen to know
wo? where?
Woche week; **wöchentlich** weekly
Wochentag weekday
Wolle wool
wollen to want
Wort word
Wurst, Würstchen sausage
Würstchenbude see *Imbiß* p. 9
Würstelstand see 'Where to Eat' p. 10

Wurstsalat see 'Regional Dishes' p. 67
Wurstwaren sausages, salami
Würze seasoning, spice; **würzen** to season

zäh hard
zahlen to pay; **Zahlung** pay, paying
Zahn tooth; **Zahnarzt** dentist; **Zahnstocher** toothpick
Zander freshwater fish of the perch family
Zander mit Meerrettichkruste see 'Regional Dishes' p. 65
zart tender
zeigen to show
Zeit time
Zeitung newspaper
Zentrum center; **zentral** central
Ziege goat; **Ziegenkäse** goast's cheese; **Ziegenmilch** goat`s milk
Zigarette cigarette; **Zigarre** cigar
Zigeuner gypsy
Zigeunerart see 'Gastronomic Terms' p. 42

Zigeunerschnitzel see 'National Dishes' p. 55

Zigeunerspieß see 'National Dishes' p. 46

Zimmer room

Zimt cinnamon

Zitrone lemon; Zitronenlimonade lemonade

Zitrusfrucht citrus fruit

zubereiten to prepare

Zucchini zucchini, courgettes

Zucht farm

Zucker sugar; Zuckerdose sugar bowl

Zuckerguß icing

zuckerkrank diabetic

Zug train

Zuger Kirschtorte see 'Sweets, Cakes and Pastries' p. 37

Zuger Rötel see 'National Dishes' p. 59

Zunge tongue

Zürcher Leberspießli, Züri Gschnätzlets see 'National Dishes' p. 59

Zürich Zurich

zurück back; zurückkommen to return

zusammen together

Zusatz added

zuschauen to watch

zu viel too much

zweite second

Zwetschge plum

Zwetschgendatschi, Zwetschgenkuchen Zwetschgenknödel see 'Sweets, Cakes and Pastries' p. 37

Zwetschgensuppe see 'Regional Dishes' p. 64

Zwiebel onion

Zwiebel gefüllt see 'Regional Dishes' p. 62

Zwiebelkuchen, -suppe see 'National Dishes' p. 56

zwischen between

Zwischenmahlzeit snack

INDEX

INTRODUCTION	3
WHERE TO EAT	8
SAUSAGES AND COLD CUTS	13
CHEESES	17
DRINKS	20
SWEETS, CAKES AND PASTRIES	29
GASTRONOMIC TERMS	38
NATIONAL DISHES	43
REGIONAL DISHES	60
RECIPES	75
ALPHABET	92
CAKESHOPS	93
CHILDREN	94
COFFEE	95
COMPLAINTS	97
CONVERSATION	98
CURRENCY	99
DATES AND CALENDAR	100
DIRECTIONS	101
EATING OUT	102
EATING OUT - Drinks	108
EATING OUT - Information	109
EATING OUT - Reservations	110
EATING OUT - Various requests	111
EMERGENCIES	112
ENTERTAINMENT	113
FOOD SHOPPING	114
GRAMMAR	115
GREETINGS	120
HOTEL	121
NUMBERS	123
PAYING THE BILL	124
PROBLEMS	125
PRONUNCIATION	126
PUBLIC HOLIDAYS	127
QUESTIONS	129
RESTROOMS	130
SMOKING	131
TAXIS	132
TELEPHONE	133
TIME	136
WEIGHTS AND MEASURES	138
DICTIONARY OF GASTRONOMIC TERMS	139

Langenscheidt's Pocket Menu Readers
are also available for the following countries:

France

Greece

Italy

Portugal & Brazil

Spain